Place Me With Your Son

The publication of this volume has been made possible in part by a generous grant from the Jesuit Community at Boston College.

Place Me With Your Son

THIRD EDITION

Ignatian Spirituality in Everyday Life

THE SPIRITUAL EXERCISES ARRANGED
AS A 24-WEEK RETREAT IN 4 PHASES
ACCORDING TO THE 19TH ANNOTATION

JAMES W. SKEHAN, S.J.

GEORGETOWN UNIVERSITY PRESS / WASHINGTON, D.C.

This volume is an extensively revised and enlarged edition of the 1985 and 1986 editions that were prepared for Jesuits and the Laity by James A. Devereux, S.J., Hugh Kennedy, S.J., Clement J. Petrik, S.J., and Terrence Toland, S.J., and with generous assistance by other members of the Maryland Province of the Society of Jesus.

Georgetown University Press, Washington, D.C.   20007–1079

Copyright © 1991 by Georgetown University Press. All rights reserved.
First edition published 1985.   Third edition 1991.
PRINTED IN THE UNITED STATES OF AMERICA
10 9 8 7 6 5
THIS VOLUME IS PRINTED ON ACID-FREE ∞ OFFSET BOOK PAPER.

Library of Congress Cataloging-in-Publication Data.

Skehan, James W.
    Place me with your son : Ignatian spirituality in everyday life
retreat / by James W. Skehan, S.J.—Rev. and enl. ed.
    p.   cm.
    1. Ignatius, of Loyola. Saint. 1491–1556. Exercitia spiritualia.
2. Spiritual exercises. I. Title.
BX2179.L8S56 1991   248.3—dc20   91-13226
ISBN 0-87840-525-9 (pbk : alk. paper)

Contents

Preface to the Third Edition

The format of these retreat guidelines to Ignatian Spirituality in Everyday Life (ISEL) relies first of all on the second edition of *Place Me With Your Son: The Spiritual Exercises in Everyday Life*, which was published in 1986. That edition was a revision of the 1985 edition which was also prepared for and by the Jesuits of the Maryland Province.

In the intervening years I have added to, subtracted from, and modified the contents of the second edition while directing "Nineteenth Annotation" retreats for and with fellow Jesuits and fellow Christians. I was stimulated to do these revisions by William J. Horne, Lecturer, School of Management at Boston College, who transcribed the entire book in a Macintosh computer draft, complete with those texts that were referenced in the *Exercises* .

The original annotations or suggestions, made by St. Ignatius in his own text of the *Spiritual Exercises*, recommend that these "exercises" be adapted to the circumstances of the person engaged in them. A modern version of the Annotations suggests that "a retreatant of talent and proper disposition" who wishes to make the full Exercises, may do so "in the face of normal occupations and living conditions for the extent of the whole retreat." Thus, one who is unable to spend a month in solitude may devote one and one-half hours daily to the Exercises over a much longer period of time. In the annual retreat which I direct at Boston College, I usually choose a beginning time such that meditations on the birth of Jesus and his Passion and Resurrection coincide approximately with the feasts of Christmas and Easter, respectively. Such a retreat, however, may be undertaken at any time.

Into this edition of *Place Me With Your Son* I have also incorporated some exercises of awareness patterned on Eastern or Buddhist meditation practices as well as devotional exercises similar to or drawn from those in *Sadhana* by Anthony de Mello, S.J. Additionally I have incorporated material from the writings of Pierre Teilhard de Chardin, S.J., drawn mainly from the *Divine Milieu*.

I am grateful to many colleagues at Boston College who have spread the word of the availability of this spiritual marathon, and especially to William A. Barry, S.J., and James M. Collins, S.J., Rector and Minister of the Jesuit Community at Boston College who hosted these retreats. I thank those who formed the several retreat groups since 1986, and whose sharing of experience in prayer has helped me in the preparation of this book. I am also grateful to Janet E. Blakeley, John B. Breslin, S.J., Patrice La Liberté, and Joseph E. O'Connor, S.J., whose editorial skills have provided me with excellent guidance. I thank also my assistant, Patricia C. Tassia who, like Martha in the Gospel, was occupied with the innumerable details necessary for the manuscript to reach the final stages, and that without complaint. Any deficiencies in this volume, however, I must claim as my own responsibility. To serve as director of these retreats continues to be one of the most rewarding experiences of my life as a Jesuit priest-scientist.

JAMES W. SKEHAN, S.J.

Boston College, 1991
The 500th Anniversary of the birth of Ignatius

Acknowledgments

THE PHILLIPS COLLECTION for the cover art: *Christ and the High Priest*, by Georges Rouault, reproduced in full color with the kind permission of The Phillips Collection, Washington, D.C.

The following publishers have generously given permission for the use of extended quotations from their copyrighted works:

DANIEL BERRIGAN for "The Face of Christ" in *The World for Wedding Ring* by Daniel Berrigan. Copyright by Daniel Berrigan, S.J., 1958, 1959, 1960, 1961, 1962, 1982. Reprinted with permission.

CENTRUM IGNATIANUM SPIRITUALITATIS for excerpts from *The Spiritual Journal of Saint Ignatius Loyola*, translated by William J. Young. Reprinted with permission of the Centrum Ignatianum Spiritualitatis, Rome.

CONFRATERNITY OF CHRISTIAN DOCTRINE for scripture texts in this work which are taken from the New American Bible with Revised New Testament, copyright 1986 by the Confraternity of Christian Doctrine, Washington, D.C.

HARCOURT BRACE JOVANOVICH for "The dove descending" from "Little Gidding" in *Four Quartets* by T.S. Eliot (seq. num. 21712), copyright 1943 by T.S. Eliot; renewed 1971 by Esmé Valerie Eliot. Reprinted by permission of Harcourt Brace Jovanovich.

INTRODUCTION TO THE SPIRITUAL EXERCISES

Guidelines for Ignatian Spirituality in Everyday Life (ISEL)

Saint Ignatius Loyola recognized that not everyone who wanted to make the Spiritual Exercises for thirty days had the leisure or the resources to do so. There were men and women who possessed the necessary qualities of mind and heart and were drawn by God to the Exercises, but were tied down by personal commitments and the press of affairs. In Annotation [19] of his text, Ignatius says that such a person "may take an hour and a half daily to exercise himself." He does not say how long the whole process will last, but he does note that the same order of the four Phases ("Weeks" in Ignatius *Autograph*) should be observed as in the book of the *Exercises* itself. This alternative method assumes that a director familiar with the Exercises will be there to guide the exercitant.

Place Me With Your Son is intended as a companion and guide to the dual text of *The Spiritual Exercises of St. Ignatius: A Literal Translation and A Contemporary Reading* by David L. Fleming S.J. It is important to have these two books for this spiritual journey. Two other companion books, each of a quite different type, are highly recommended but are not essential for carrying out the Exercises. The first is *Sadhana: A Way to God—Christian Exercises in Eastern Form* by de Mello. The other is *The Divine Milieu* by Teilhard de Chardin. The specific usefulness of each is outlined in the subsection on written resources.

There are genuine advantages to be gained from making the Spiritual Exercises in the way suggested in Annotation [19]. Such an experience strengthens the habit of regular prayer, teaches a greater facility in discernment, increases one's sense of the presence of God, and helps to integrate prayer and work. But there are also drawbacks.

NOTES: The bracketed numbers [1] through [20] identify the first twenty Annotations as originally enumerated by Ignatius, and numbers [21] through [370] traditionally count the remainder of the text of the *Exercises*.

The dual text of the *Exercises* referred to above is particularly useful. It consists of an exact, faithful rendering made in 1909 by Elder Mullan, S.J., of the sixteenth-century Spanish *Autograph* and of a parallel twentieth-century interpretation completed in 1977 by Fleming. Before 1909, most users of the *Exercises* had to rely on translations variously made from Latin translations of the original.

J.W.S.

It is difficult to set aside that much time each day; a director may not be readily available; written guides to Ignatian Spirituality in Everyday Life (ISEL) are better understood in discussion with a director. It is hoped that this text, without presuming to eliminate every difficulty, will make it easier to follow the Spiritual Exercises and so to enjoy their blessing in everyday life.

Time Allotted for the Exercises

According to the directive of Ignatius for one "who is more disengaged" [20], the full Exercises are usually completed in about thirty consecutive days. But for those "taken up with public affairs or suitable business," the course is extended over twenty-four weeks. However, Ignatius also refers to his major time divisions within the Exercises as "Weeks" although each consists of three or more weeks. In order to avoid confusion in this retreat I substitute the term "Phase" to refer to these four major divisions. "Week" in this third edition is thus reserved for the time interval of seven days. Moreover, because of the length of this "Annotation 19" retreat, I have found it helpful to note beginning dates on a Calendar for the Spiritual Exercises. That calendar may be found on the last page of this book.

Annotation [19] speaks of taking an hour and a half daily for the Spiritual Exercises. This includes not only time for prayer but also for preparation and reflection, and participation in Mass if possible. Since the commitments of active Christians are heavy, some may not be able to give this much time to the Exercises. Others may be able to give more. Moreover, some may wish to divide the time so as to spend two periods a day in prayer. Whatever one's situation, all will want to make some sacrifice of time during these months in order to respond more generously to God's invitation.

Freedom to Follow God's Promptings

Some who use this text may feel the need to give more or less time to the content of one phase in preference to another. In this, as in all things, one should exercise the freedom of the children of God and follow the promptings of his grace.

It will be helpful from time to time to refer to the guidelines and methods that Ignatius offers as Aids for Prayer [73-90, 5, 21, 22, 24-32, and 43].

The Director of the Exercises

Ignatius suggests that "the director of the Exercises, as a balance at equilibrium, without leaning toward one side or another, should permit the Creator to deal directly with the creature, and the creature directly with his Creator and Lord" [15M].* For Ignatius, therefore, God himself is the director. Nevertheless, the human instrument may explain the process of the Exercises, give instruction in prayer, assist in discerning the various spirits, validate the exercitant's graces and propose further matter for prayer.

Perhaps the most important function of the director is to require of the exercitant a certain accountability in prayer, and so lessen the distortion that can come from the evil spirit and confirm those graces that come from God. A conversation with one's spiritual director will help to discover which of the following modes of accountability is best for you:

1. One may invite a trusted and respected person to be a director in the full sense—one who will assume responsibility for all the functions assigned by Ignatius to the director in the Guidelines or, as they were originally called, "Annotations."

2. One may continue to hold regular meetings with a spiritual director, but the conversations focus on the progress of the Exercises in Everyday Life and are more frequent than they would be in ordinary circumstances.

3. Two exercitants may meet with each other every week in order to engage in spiritual conversation about the Exercises and to share with one another how God has been leading them in prayer. In this mode each partner, not strictly the director of the other, agrees to be accountable to the other in helping to discover God's ways.

4. Small groups of exercitants, generally ten or fewer, agree to meet regularly so as to share with each other what has been happening in their prayer, and thus act as instruments of God's grace for one another as they engage in the Exercises. This is the format that I use at Boston College, where we meet once a week for three and one-half hours—for Mass, dinner, guidance for the following week's prayer, shared experience of the previous week's prayer, and a guided meditation to conclude. This meeting format is one that I personally favor because it provides the possibility of a powerful group dynamic, once a level of trust has been achieved. Additionally a private meeting with one's spiritual director from time to time helps provide valuable insights to progress. This mode commonly results in the formation of

---

* Numbered guidelines from the text of the *Exercises* followed by the letter "M" indicate modification(s) or change(s) that I have introduced.

J.W.S.

a post-retreat prayer group or in some instances, a Christian Life Community.

5. One may make the Exercises privately, setting aside an hour each week to review the graces granted by God and to keep some record of the various movements of the soul.

With great wisdom Ignatius provides a guideline that the director and the retreatant always put a favorable interpretation on each other's statements so as to avoid misinterpretation and so that a correct understanding may develop [22]. This "plus sign," as Jesuits often call it, is a recommendation that, if followed, would undoubtedly produce harmony and goodwill worldwide.

Written Resources for an ISEL Retreat

Place Me With Your Son contains introductory suggestions concerning a suitable "attitude" with which one may approach the prayer period; "the gift or grace" that one ardently desires throughout the entire week; and a brief description of "the setting" for the meditations based generally on Scriptural passages; all leading up to the "colloquy" or "conversation" with God and/or our Mother, Mary. Some may find it helpful to read and to pray in the spirit of religious poems that capture some of the flavor of the particular week's meditations. Certainly, St. Ignatius encourages us to engage the imagination and the feelings in our conversation with the Lord.

Obviously, the first companion resource to *Place Me With Your Son* is a good edition of the *Spiritual Exercises* itself. As explained earlier, I have selected Fleming's version, *The Spiritual Exercises of St. Ignatius: A Literal Translation and A Contemporary Reading,* as eminently suitable. Or one may use Fleming's *Contemporary Reading of the Spiritual Exercises.* Published later by Doubleday, it does not carry Mullan's literal translation as a parallel text. Either of these companion volumes will help one to understand the Exercises better and to pray over them more readily. Louis Puhl's translation of the *Exercises* is also a very readable English version.

The essential resource is, of course, the Holy Bible. (Scriptural quotations in this edition are from *The New American Bible (NAB) with Revised New Testament.*) A mini-commentary on the biblical text is contained in footnotes to the NAB. Two other, new commentaries on the Bible are *The New Jerome Biblical Commentary* and *The Collegeville Bible Commentary.* While such commentaries may be helpful in many respects, they are not necessary for carrying out the Spiritual Exercises fruitfully.

Although not strictly essential to the Retreat, I recommend de Mello's *Sadhana* since it contains exercises of awareness patterned on Eastern or Buddhist meditation practice as well as fantasy and other devotional exercises. Additionally, Teilhard de Chardin's little book, *The Divine Milieu*, offers a rich, far from traditional but, I believe, authentic approach to Ignatian spirituality. Also, a list of other written resources for the Exercises may be found on pages 163 to 165 of this book.

A final indispensable resource is an easily portable notebook, wherein regular reflections on daily prayer can be recorded as one's "journal." For an example of St. Ignatius' own written reflections on his life of prayer, see *The Spiritual Journal of St. Ignatius Loyola*, translated by William J. Young, S.J.

Structures of Daily Prayer

A day of the ISEL Retreat forms a solid basis for one's life as a contemplative in action. There is time for daily prayer, for daily worship and for the daily examen. But during the Exercises we would wish to offer to God and to each other the gifts of greater intensity in prayer, greater awareness of God's presence, greater fidelity. Each retreatant is asked to pray with and for the communities that are of greatest importance in one's life, including others of the Retreat group.

The daily Eucharist is the immediate source of one's life. During the Exercises one is asked to make a conscious effort to link the liturgy with the themes of the retreat insofar as this is possible without contrivance. During the petitions of the Mass we should pray fervently for the retreat group that each may be enlightened and enlivened by the Holy Spirit.

During the daily examination of consciousness one may wish to reflect on the Exercises of that day and also on how one's prayer is integrated with one's work and ministry as a disciple of the Lord (see p. 12 of this book).

A weekly reflection on our prayer according to one of the modes of accountability described earlier in the subsection, The Director, is essential to the dynamic of the Ignatian Exercises in everyday life. Questions and topics that may be raised during that reflection are given below in treating of the daily reflection after prayer.

Some Ignatian Forms of Prayer

In the *Spiritual Exercises* Ignatius outlines three Methods of Praying when resources, such as a text of Scripture, are not at hand. He provides simple directives to help us in using them [238-60]. For each of these three, he describes the Preparation, the Grace sought, the Method, and he ends with the Colloquy or intimate conversation with God our Lord.

The First Method of Praying deals with the ten commandments [239-43], the seven deadly sins [244-45], the three powers of the soul [246], and the five senses of the body [247-48].

The Second Method of Praying centers on contemplating the meaning of each word in a traditional prayer formula [249-57].

The Third Method of Praying is a modification of the Second Method, and consists of making use of such prayer formulas but in a less ponderous manner [258-60]. It recommends that one be so relaxed that breathing in and out takes place at a slow but steady pace, so that each word of a prayer formula can be said and reflected upon during a single in-and-out cycle.

Historical Roots of Ignatian Spirituality

Ignatian spirituality has strong historical links to twelfth century Cistercian and Carthusian traditions. David Stanley, S.J., cites one of the clearest Carthusian statements as it is found in Guigo's "prayer ladder." By it one may rise by grace and free will to the heights of prayer: "There are four rungs to 'Guigo's ladder': *lectio*, the attentive, reverent Reading of Scripture; *meditatio*, the diligent Mental Reflection upon the truth hidden in the reading; *oratio*, persevering Appeal for Divine Help in achieving communion with God; and *contemplatio*, the Fruit of God's Compassionate Response by which the devout heart is raised to Himself through consolation." (*I Encountered God*, p.11). The distinction between meditation and contemplation in the mind of Ignatius, lies in the experience of "consolation," [316–17] a quaint phrase meaning a reaction in prayer, which together with its opposite, "desolation" is the keystone of the Spiritual Exercises.

MEDITATION is discursive prayer that employs the three faculties of the soul: memory, intellect, and will. Ignatius explains his understanding of meditation in the First Point of the Exercises of the First Phase [50]. He does not mean that the exercitant is to apply the faculties of the soul in order, one by one. Rather, they all work together, but the primacy belongs to the will, which has the first and last word. The subject matter of meditation is not abstract truth but the concrete realities of faith. In meditation we seek not simply to comprehend these realities intellectually but to savor them interiorly. Thus, the movement of this form of prayer is towards contemplation, that is toward the love of God, a love which is given intimate expression in the COLLOQUY. This form of prayer may be described as "friend speaking to friend."

Ignatius often uses contemplation and meditation as equivalents, but contemplation usually has as its SETTING (or subject matter) "an episode of the Gospel, on which the gaze of the soul can pause, dwell, and find delight" (Brou, *Ignatian Methods of Prayer*, p. 130). Ignatius gives us a concrete example of contemplation in the exercise on the Nativity [110-17]. Here, as in every Ignatian contemplation, we dwell on the persons, the words and the action of the Gospel text because they disclose the mystery of Christ the Lord, who died and rose again and is living still in His Church. We ourselves enter into that mystery heart and soul. Indeed, it is completed in us as members of the Lord's Body.

"REPETITIONS" and the "APPLICATION OF THE SENSES" are both characteristic of the cyclical Ignatian method. (Ignatius usually presents his exercises of prayer in cycles of five.) The First and the Second Exercises offer new matter which the exercitant must work at with some effort. The Third and the Fourth are Repetitions and the Fifth Exercise is an Application of the Senses. The movement over these five exercises is from very active prayer which engages me vigorously to more receptive prayer in which I can peacefully allow the Lord to love me. Fleming "reads" or interprets Ignatius' directions in this way:

> Rather than take up new subject matter for consideration, I should return to those thoughts and feelings which struck me forcefully from the First and Second Exercises. I review those areas in which I felt greater consolation or desolation or, in general, greater spiritual appreciation. The idea of repetition is to let sink further into my heart the movements of God through the means of subject matter already presented [62].

> [The Fourth Exercise] is meant to be a repetition again— sometimes called a summary or résumé. The hope is that the mind becomes less and less active with ideas since the subject matter does not change, and as a result the heart is more and more central to the way I find myself responding. The prayer period will probably be less active on one hand, and yet on the other, by the grace of God it will grow in intensity [64].

> [The Application of the Senses] is meant to be my own "letting go", a total immersion of myself into the mystery of Christ's life this day. . . . it is not a matter of thinking new thoughts or of trying new methods of getting into the mystery. Rather the notion is to build upon all the experiences which have been part of my prayer day. Again it is akin to the passive way my senses take in sights, smells, sounds, feelings, as an automatic datum for my attention. The total felt-environment of the particular mystery of Christ's life, in whatever ways it can be most vividly mine, is the setting for the final period of prayer in each day [122-25].

Preparation for Prayer

The preparation for prayer takes fifteen minutes or less. It has to do with basic decisions and basic attitudes. During this period of preparation one decides where to pray, the posture that one will take in prayer, when and how long one will pray, and the subject of prayer. Normally this last, the subject, will be one of the scriptural texts or texts in the Exercises suggested for that particular phase. The basic attitude in preparation for prayer is reverence. Reverence acknowledges that God is present to me and governs my physical and psychic comportment accordingly. Ignatius tells us to begin every exercise with a Preparatory Prayer in which I direct all that I am and all that I do during that time to the praise and glory of the Divine Majesty. *The preparatory prayer is never omitted.*

The Prayer Itself

Two things happen in prayer: what I do and what is done to me. The first is under my control and the second is beyond it. There are many things that I can control when I pray. I may read Scripture, listen to the words of Jesus, reason on the truths of Revelation, make acts of faith, hope, love, petition, gratitude, praise. I may be quiet and listen. I may sing hymns and recite psalms, I may finger my rosary or pray the Stations of the Cross. I may engage in what Ignatius calls meditation and contemplation.

The second aspect of prayer is what happens to me when I pray. In Annotation [15] Ignatius assumes that while one is engaged in the Spiritual Exercises our Creator and Lord can communicate himself in person to the devout soul, and that He will inflame it with his love and praise, and dispose it for the way in which it could better serve him in the future. Ignatius teaches us to reflect on our experiences of prayer so that we may discern the various movements of the spirits: movements of grace in which we are drawn towards God, movements of the evil spirit in which we are led away from Him.

The meditations and contemplations of the Exercises are always pointed towards the Grace or Gift that I Seek and the Colloquy with the Lord. Grace in this sense is something that I do not have that I really want and that only God can give. I do not bring it about in myself; I can ask for it, wait for it, accept it, or reject it. The Graces that Ignatius bids us ask for are all affective graces, things to be felt and experienced. In each prayer of the Exercises we are to persist in begging God for these gifts. The Colloquy aims at establishing and confirming a personal relationship between the exercitant and Mary, God the Father, Jesus, and the holy Spirit. It is in such a relationship

that we ought to pray. The more the Colloquy pervades the entire period of prayer, the more we grow in personal relationship with God
and are disposed to receive what He wishes to give us. The various
points and considerations for prayer are meant to help us develop
dispositions that will enable us to enter into a loving relationship
with the Lord.

Ignatius encourages us to persevere in the period of prayer that
we set ourselves and not to lengthen it or shorten it. Fidelity to prayer
in a dry season is often blessed with sudden grace. Ignatius also tells
us to bring the formal prayer to a clear or definite conclusion by recit-
ing the Lord's Prayer or some other familiar vocal prayer.

Reflection on Prayer

In his "reading" of *The Spiritual Exercises,* Fleming interprets Ignatius' instructions about reflection on prayer, in the following way
[77]:

1. After a formal prayer period is finished, I should review
what has happened during the past hour—not so much what
ideas I had, but more the movements of consolation, desolation,
fear, anxiety, boredom, and so on, and perhaps something about
my distractions, especially if they were deep or disturbing. I thank
God for His favors and ask pardon for my own negligences of the
prayer time. Often it is good to signalize the difference of this review of prayer from the prayer period itself by some change of
place or position.

2. I should spend about fifteen minutes in such a review. I
may find it very helpful to jot down some of the various reflections that strike me so that I can more easily discuss with my director what has been my progress from prayer period to prayer
period.

It is important to make this written reflection and review immediately after prayer, and to use it as the basis for the weekly account of
one's progress in the Exercises.

Guidelines for the Discernment of Spirits

"Discernment of spirits" is a venerable phrase in the Christian
spiritual tradition [313-36]. From the action of good or evil spirits
upon one, result "movements of one's heart or spirit", "motions af-
fecting one's interior life", "a certain impetus in one's life", "a feeling
for or against some course of action", and so on. Since such discernment is at the heart of Ignatian spirituality, it will be a recurring consideration throughout the several phases of the Exercises. Because of

their importance to the process of discernment of spirits, special mention is made of spiritual consolation [316, 323-27] and of spiritual desolation [317-22].

Awareness Meditation and Its Relation to Ignatian Prayer

Eastern awareness meditation or "centering" forms of prayer, may differ from the Ignatian types discussed above, but I believe that awareness discipline is not only basic to, but presupposed in the Ignatian method. Additionally I believe that it is an important path to contemplation as defined above. Contemplation may be regarded as communication with God that makes a minimal use of words, images, and concepts or dispenses with them altogether. This is the sort of prayer that John of the Cross speaks of in his writing about the dark night of the soul or the author of *The Cloud of Unknowing* explains in his admirable book.

Mystics have told us that, in addition to the mind and the heart with which we ordinarily communicate with God, we are all endowed with a mystical mind and a mystical heart—together a faculty which makes it possible for us to know God directly, to grasp and intuit him in his very being, though in a dark manner, apart from thoughts, concepts, and images. In most of us this "Heart" lies deep asleep and undeveloped. If it were to be awakened it would be constantly straining toward God and, given a chance, would draw our whole being toward him. But for this, it needs to be developed, it needs to have the dross that surrounds it removed so that it can be attracted toward the "Eternal Magnet."

Notice how sharp is the hearing and the sense of touch of the blind person. Having lost the faculty of seeing, such a person has been forced to develop other faculties of perception. Something similar happens in the mystical world. If we could go mentally blind, so to speak, or if we could blindfold our mind while we are communicating with God, we would be forced to develop some other faculty for communicating with him—that faculty which, according to a number of mystics, is already straining to move out to him anyway if it were given a chance to develop—the heart.

If you would communicate with God through this heart that the mystics speak of, you must first silence the mind. Awareness meditations, such as those in *Sadhana*, are an excellent way to attain to this silence of spirit. Even in your prayer time try gently to reduce the amount of thinking that you do and pray more with the heart. Saint Teresa of Avila used to say, "The important thing is not to think much but to love much." So do a lot of loving during your time of prayer. And God will guide you even though it be through a period of trial and error.

Consciousness Examen or Christian Insight Meditation

Ignatius considered the "examen" to be a form of prayer that is of paramount importance among spiritual exercises. Unfortunately, this exercise has been much misunderstood as being a relatively sterile method of self improvement, and one having narrowly moralistic overtones. As such, the exercise can not only be an unsatisfactory kind of prayer, but may also become a source of dissatisfaction with all spiritual exercises as well as a source of guilt. For many who are otherwise well versed in the Spiritual Exercises, "Examen" suggests the examination of conscience associated with confession, tabulation of sins, and assignment of guilt. Indeed, for some the term "examen" carries distasteful emotional overtones that undermine the practice it is meant to foster. So Aschenbrenner introduced the term "Consciousness Examen" to capture and amplify upon the spirit of Ignatius' practice, distinguishing between it and the examen of conscience. Fleming's comments (pp. 61, 63) on the Guidelines of Ignatius [24-43] reflect an outlook on this practice similar to Aschenbrenner's refreshing approach.

For this same prayer form, I use the new term "Christian Insight Meditation" or CIM, that I and many of my retreatants have found helpful since it carries no emotional baggage. I adapt CIM from Buddhist Insight Meditation practice. That practice is an exercise of discernment of interior movements in one's daily life with much in common with the Ignatian examen. I suggest that you use whatever assists you best in reaching the goals of the practice.

In any case, the examen should not be an exercise of unhealthy self-centered introspection, but an exercise of awareness to observe the "movement of spirits." Thus one may develop a kind of detached awareness of and sensitivity to the intimately special ways that the Spirit of the Lord has for uniquely approaching and calling each one. This insight may foster a growing spirit of love and sense of special providence, truly a gift of the Spirit.

Ignatius encourages us to become progressively more aware of two contrasting spontaneities or movements in our consciousness: one that is good and from God, and another that is evil and not from God. He further encourages us to cultivate or to nullify each of these "spirits" according to our insights. When examen is related to discernment, it becomes an examen *of consciousness* rather than *of conscience*, the latter having narrow moralistic overtones. Again, I refer to this kind of prayer as Christian Insight Meditation or CIM. In its practice, our concern is not primarily with the morality of good or bad actions, but rather with how the Lord affects us and moves us, commonly quite spontaneously and in the depths of our consciousness. This divine magnetism is referred to in John's Gospel when

Jesus says "No one can come to me unless the Father who sent me draw him" (Jn 6:44).

The goal is that we may be free enough to yield to that heartfelt spontaneity and divine magnetism by which the Father draws us to Himself, and by which the Holy Spirit anoints us with His wisdom and love.

Format for the Practice of Christian Insight Meditation (CIM)

The following is a much abridged version of the consciousness examination that Aschenbrenner put into a form suitable for insight meditation during a retreat. Thus, no matter what limitations may impede carrying out the Exercises, one should set aside time to pray for enlightenment, to give thanks, to review the day for signs of God's presence and his gifts, for contrition and for joyous optimism for the next period of prayer. The CIM method is summarized here for you:

1. Take a moment to become interiorly quiet either through regular breathing or through focusing of attention. For example, gaze at a lighted candle, or at the tabernacle, a tree or a flower or the like—or merely close your eyes and Pray for Insight, for Enlightenment.

2. A prayer of Gratitude for being—for being here—and for all of life's gifts.

3. Ask God for what you desire. Here ask for the Grace to detect the Presence of God in the Past Day (or Half Day) as you survey that period of time as follows: Recall the events of the day hour by hour or period by period and note how you felt and what happened. Were there moments when you felt something significant taking place? Without being overly systematic let memories of the past day or so arise spontaneously, trusting that God's holy spirit will push to the surface the important events. Do you have a sense that God was present at any of these moments or times?

4. Contrition and Sorrow naturally flow from the previous parts, as you grow in realization of the Father's awesome desire that you love him with all your being.

5. Hopeful Resolution for the Future is a discernment process in which you honestly examine and evaluate your hope or your discouragement in looking to the future and in trying to become aware of the ways in which the Lord is revealing himself to you. With St. Paul you may say, "I leave the past behind and with hands outstretched to whatever lies ahead, I go straight for the goal." End with the Lord's Prayer.

PREPARATION FOR PHASE ONE PRAYER

The "How" and "Why" of the Exercises

Historical Background of the Author

Inigo of Loyola was born into a noble Basque family in 1491. A young man with a fiery temper, he became a soldier and was much preoccupied with a romantic love of chivalry. At age 26 he was badly wounded in a battle with the French at Pamplona in Spain, when a cannon ball crushed one leg and seriously wounded the other. Subsequently he was moved to the family castle of Loyola in northern Spain where he suffered two excruciating operations to set the compound fractures of his shattered leg. He underwent the second painful operation so that he could walk and dance and continue to be the handsome and engaging figure that he had been before his wartime injury.

During his long convalescence he engaged in two sets of vivid daydreams. In the first he dreamed of performing great chivalrous deeds and so winning the favor of a great lady, possibly a princess. These prolonged daydreams gave him great delight. Lacking more interesting reading, he also read the life of Christ and a book of the lives of the saints. As a result he found that he was inspired to dream of following Christ in great hardship and of imitating the saints. These aspirations also gave him great delight. One day, however, he noticed that there was a difference in his experience of these vastly different daydreams. Ignatius, speaking of himself in the third person as autobiographer, tells us in his journal of these significant personal insights:

> When he [Inigo] was thinking of the things of the world he was filled with delight, but when afterwards he dismissed them from weariness, he was dry and dissatisfied. And when he thought of going barefoot to Jerusalem and of eating nothing but herbs and performing the other rigors he saw that the saints had performed, he was consoled, not only when he entertained these thoughts, but even after dismissing them he remained cheerful and satisfied. . . .Thus, step by step, he came to recognize the difference between the two spirits that moved him, the one being from the evil spirit, the other from God (Young, 1974, p.100).

Ignatius' constant search, from the days of his convalescence at Loyola, was to put order into his life. He now realized that the first thing necessary was to know the purpose for which he had been created. What mattered most of all was to fulfill God's design for him. To do God's will it was necessary, above all, to know it. The obstacle was to be found in the "disordered affections" which obscure the eyes of the mind and drag the will toward sin. He would have to fight against these disordered affections, and for this he would have to overcome himself. This was the end to which the *Exercises* would be a help, and in their title he synthesizes their whole content: "Spiritual Exercises to overcome oneself and to order one's life without making one's decision through some affection which is disordered."

It is in confrontation with God's plans that sin, the creature's rebellion, arises. Inigo reviewed in his mind the course of his life, recalling the sins committed from year to year, the houses where he had lived, his dealings with others, the offices he had exercised. Two feelings overpowered his soul, shame and sorrow: shame for the loathsomeness of his sins, sorrow for having offended God. But the result was not despair. "Imagine Christ our Lord before you on the cross, and begin a colloquy with him. Ponder how it is that from being Creator he has come to make himself man, and to pass from eternal life to death here in time, that thus he might die for my sins. I shall also reflect on myself and ask: What have I done for Christ? What am I doing for Christ? What ought I to do for Christ?" Inigo's life will be an answer to this interrogation (de Dalmases, pp. 67-68).

Preliminary Recommendations for an ISEL Retreat

Although the materials presented in this book are considered suitable for the use of retreatants during each day of the ISEL retreat, they are resources only and are to be used only to the extent that they are helpful. Do not follow directives in these resources blindly. They are merely suggested materials for possible use by you, the retreatant. Rather place yourself in God's "hands" and let the dynamic of prayer and of God's dealing with you introduce you to the ideas of this First Phase. The resources are not meant to lead you through the Exercises, although they follow the sequence of meditations that Ignatius found to be most helpful in developing a spirit of complete generosity toward God. They are proposed as a possible help to a kind of contemplative prayer that involves looking at the Lord and what he has done.

Thus I suggest that during these weeks you meditate on Psalms 103, 104, and 105 and any others, that may provide a pattern for your prayer to God in praise and thanksgiving for all that he has done. For instance, look at the flowers, the hills, trees, sunlight, rain. Smell them, feel them, hear them, and then let the response well up in your heart. In other words I encourage you to pray spontaneously, to enjoy this kind of prayer, and to find your own way and content. If the attached materials are helpful, use them; but if the Lord moves you in directions other than in making use of these pages, follow the Lord and the Spirit. If you come to the retreat with a "problem" to be solved or a decision to be made, place it on "Hold" for a while, and just look at the Lord and react to Him. You may confidently let the Lord lead you as to when to take up a problem or decision.

Once you get deep enough into what we might call a "first phase experience," that is, after you have been praying in praise and thanksgiving for some time, after basking in the consolation of the Lord for two or three weeks, you may begin to experience a sense of alienation, of spiritual impotence, of desolation. Previously you may have found the Psalms full of praise and hardly noted the references to sinfulness or to the futility of poorly motivated human hopes. Now these references may take center stage in your attention. You may feel desolate, unable to return to the consolation of the past few weeks, and alienated from God. You may even begin to doubt the experience of the past few weeks and to question whether you have ever been able to really pray. You will feel yourself unworthy of God.

If you have at this stage a sense of helplessness and hopelessness, a feeling of being lost and lonely, of having botched your life, you may be sure that you are being led by the Lord and your own needs to recognize and even to experience a feeling of your sinfulness. This experience is an experience in the present, not just a memory. You may experience yourself as alienated and desolate *now*, as needy *now*. At times this experience can be frightening and deeply distasteful. Nevertheless, do not seek to escape this experience prematurely but face it, and confront the reality of your sinfulness. Each retreatant's experience of alienation is unique and is influenced by his/her past and present. Each of us has a personal history of sin.

From Desolation to God's Healing Love

You may be confident that the Spirit will lift you from this desolation at the right moment if you are able to open yourself up to the healing love of God. If you stay with your feelings of desolation until you are ready to turn to the Lord for help, especially to Jesus who died for us sinners, then you will truly be able to experience the "good news" that he proclaims. It may take some weeks to arrive at this experience, but it will be well worth the patient work that is required. Many retreatants experience tears of joy as they understand themselves to be loved sinners. For many the experience is like a baptism, a conversion, a new birth; this knowledge is deep and abiding and leads to action and desire, the kind of knowing that seeks to be shared and spread.

It is important that you realize that by praying you will enter the dark valley without being led by anyone else but yourself and God. Most of you will experience great release and relief if you believe in the God who walks through that dark valley with you. "The effectiveness of this 'first phase' experience in the Exercises comes precisely because both the alienation and the saving are experienced in the present. In the present—and in prayer—I experience my helplessness, my alienation—those things in myself that I was running away from"—and wonder of wonders, "I find that I have nothing to fear; God loves me with all my warts and moles." This experience of sinfulness leading to the experience of salvation in turn leads to a desire to share with others the "good news"; it leads to a desire to be a follower, a companion of Jesus. When the experience has reached that stage, you are on the threshold of the Second Phase of the Spiritual Exercises" (Barry, 1973, pp. 97-100).

Guidelines that are suitable especially for the first phase are to be found in [313–27] (Fleming, 1978, p.203).

As an exercitant you will notice that in this edition of *Place Me With Your Son* all the prayers and poems are printed in italic rather than in the roman type of the text prose. This typographic differentiation was recommended to us as a simple attractive way to help you be aware that "songs of the spirit" are meant always to be spoken by you to your God—not simply read.

On the facing page you will find just such a prayer, "Soul of Christ." It has long been associated with Ignatius of Loyola and was a favorite of his. Although he was not its author, he refers to it expressly in the text of the *Exercises* in four places dealing with the colloquy and in the three methods of prayer. This prayer sums up the whole spirit and movement of the Exercises in terms of their being Christ-centered. It concentrates in every phrase on Christ's becoming our life, so that we may live only in him. Indeed, "This prayer, like the movement present in the Exercises themselves, centers us so much upon the person of Jesus Christ that, with St. Paul (Gal. 2: 20), we are meant to exclaim 'the life I live now is not my own, Christ is living in me" (Fleming, 1973, pp.3–4).

Soul of Christ

Soul of Christ, sanctify me.
Body of Christ, save me.
Blood of Christ, inebriate me.
Water from the side of Christ, wash me.
Passion of Christ, strengthen me.
O good Jesus, hear me.
Within Thy wounds hide me.
Permit me not to be separated from Thee.

From the wicked foe defend me.
At the hour of my death call me
And bid me come to Thee,
That with Thy saints I may praise Thee
For ever and ever. Amen.

PHASE ONE OF THE EXERCISES: *Weeks 1 to 4*

Week 1: *Soul of Christ, sanctify me!*

My attitude: As I enter this approximately six-month period of grace, I desire to dispose myself in a special way during the first week so as to experience the loving God as he chooses to give himself to me. To this end I recall his love and his grace in my own history and in that of my ancestors. Moreover, I am determined to seek and to find him so that he may love me anew, that I may return from exile and slavery to share more fully God's life and spirit in the land he promised.

What I seek: That I may find God in all things and always. That God may give me a more profound experience of his love, a deeper awareness of how I can respond to it, and a joyous freedom which comes from seeking God's will for me.

Day 1 of Week 1: Isaiah 43: 1–7
"I have called you by name. Fear not! I have redeemed you. You are mine!"

This beautiful poem begins and ends with the key verbs: create, form, and name; and it celebrates the return of Israel from exile as a new creation of Yahweh. This is accomplished as a result of the obligation of blood relationship. "Fear not, for I am with you. You are precious in my eyes . . . I love you." So completely do Yahweh's children share divine life that they are henceforth to be addressed by no other name than the Lord's. Today, in similar fashion, the children of God's own Son have their special name, Christian, and their Father is God, the Father, the same Yahweh who has called us by name.

Day 2 of Week 1: John 14: 16–17, 19
Finding God in All Things

The Spiritual Master met the disciple who told him that he had been searching for God for five years but had been unable to find him. "Where have you looked for him?" asked the Master. "I have searched in the desert; I have looked for him on the mountains; I have searched everywhere—in the country, in the villages, everywhere—and I have been unable to find him." What the Master knew, but the disciple had not yet learned is that God can be found anywhere—everywhere. God has a thousand eyes, a million or more faces, even though a Spirit. God can be found everywhere if one is prepared to find him. One must know, not so much where to find God but how to do so.

What must I do to discover what the Master really means by saying that God can be found anywhere and everywhere? It is a secret that Ignatius had discovered and that he wished to pass on to each of us who engage in the Spiritual Exercises. Egan's comment about Ignatius Loyola the Mystic should encourage us in our practice, because he tells us that Ignatius' "ease in finding God was always increasing. . . .At whatever time or hour he wanted to find God, he found him" (p. 60). Such a practice is central to Ignatian spirituality.

In order to find God in all things, however, I must develop new eyes so that I can peer beyond the appearances of things; I must recognize that the world of the spirit is at least as real, though not as tangible, as the physical world in which my everyday life is lived. Part of that world is within me; and part of that world is all around me. John the Evangelist speaks to this point: "I will ask the Father, and he will give you another Advocate to be with you always, the Spirit of truth which the world cannot accept, because it neither sees nor knows it; but you know him, because it remains with you, and will be in you. . . .In a little while the world will no longer see me; but you will see me." What a magnificent promise and statement of confidence that I can find and recognize the living Spirit within me (Jn 14: 16-17, 19).

Day 3 of Week 1: Awareness Meditation
A Buddhist-Christian Method of Prayer.

To learn to meditate we must learn to listen to the silent voice of the great teacher whom St. Augustine called "the Master Within." If you listen to his voice you will learn to pray. Our Judaeo-Christian tradition offers many helps to meditation and we will, of course, make use of these. But the Buddhist tradition provides us with a practice that can facilitate and enrich our Christian meditation practice. That is awareness meditation, an important practice that has profound implications for assisting our Christian prayer and for improving many aspects of everyday life as well.

Awareness meditation is a powerful means for cultivating the emotional silence necessary for satisfactory prayer. In and of itself it is not necessarily prayer, but there can be little sustained prayerfulness and actual prayer without awareness or mindfulness. Let us now begin the practice of awareness meditation and you will quickly see what I mean. Sustained practice of awareness meditation from time to time will improve the quality of your Christian meditation.

Begin this first awareness meditation by taking a comfortable posture that you can maintain without moving for the period indicated, or at least without a conscious decision to do so. This may require a bit of discipline at first, but you will come to appreciate its value as time goes on.

1. While sitting still in as deep a silence as possible for ten minutes, make your breathing in and then out the focus of your attention throughout the period, noting whether it is shallow or deep, rapid or slow, soundless or wheezing, and any other features that you become aware of. As the period progresses, does your breathing slow down perceptibly? Don't try to control your breathing—this is an awareness exercise—meant only to observe what happens not to control the results.

2. If your thoughts wander, take note of the fact and gently guide your wandering attention back to the breathing as often as necessary.

3. If you had some success in attaining interior silence such that you could focus for most of the period on the breathing, try to describe the qualities of that silence. Repeat this exercise two or three times in a row from time to time and you will become aware of an improvement in your ability to focus your mind on whatever you choose.

However, the chief importance of this exercise to your spiritual life ultimately is twofold: First, over time, as you repeat this and related breathing exercises, you will become aware that your interior silence, your ability to focus and to concentrate, will increase greatly as you let go of anxiety, fear, laziness, etc. You will gain controlled energy. Second, the important objective of this kind of exercise is to develop an awareness of what influences are operative in your mind and in your activities. You will find that increased awareness and perception will be very significant in the "discernment of spirits" and in the examination of consciousness discussed earlier in the Introduction (see page 11).

Day 4 of Week 1: Isaiah 55: 1–13
God lovingly invites me to come to Him.

I have the opportunity to come out of slavery as part of a new Exodus. Yahweh is my shepherd in this retreat, as in all of life. He is forever intent on bringing me, one of his chosen people, back to the "Promised Land" from exile and slavery. These verses from Isaiah are the conclusion to the Book of Comfort, as it is called (chaps. 40-55). Nearly every major theme here is blended into this magnificent finale. Chapter 55, an invitation to grace, comes full circle echoing many key words or themes of Chapter 40. These include a new exodus (40:1-11; 55:12-13), a new covenant (55:3); the way (40:3, 27; 55:7-9), forgiveness (40:2; 55:6-7), and a call to pasture or to eat (40:11;

55:1-2). In verse 6 the phrase, "seek the Lord", normally was used to invite people to the sanctuary but here is used to exhort Yahweh's people to seek God elsewhere as well, indeed everywhere. So I too am called to find God in all things. Verses 12 and 13 recall the Exodus theme: all the world finds peace and bursts into song as God brings Israel—and me—back from exile and slavery.

Day 5 of Week 1: Luke 12: 22–31
"If God so clothes the grass in the field that grows today and is thrown into the oven tomorrow, will he not much more provide for you!"

Jesus tells his followers, including me, to let go of worrying, to give up grasping for things that are of lesser importance, such as what I am to eat, what I am to wear, how long I am to live. Jesus looks to nature, to the ravens, to the lilies to help me to learn how I am to live my life. His message is "Stop worrying. The unbelievers of this world are always running after these things. Your Father knows that you need such things. Seek out instead his kingship over you, and the rest will follow in turn" (NAB).

It is not enough, even if I should be devout, to tell myself not to worry—I well know how "that" works at times—I must practice letting go of cares, of anger, of greed through awareness or insight meditation practice. Thus will I be able to keep the demons of worry at bay and be able with peace of mind and energy to "seek instead his Kingship. . . .and the rest will follow in turn."

Day 6 of Week 1: Psalm 104: 1–35
"O Lord, my God, you are great indeed!"

Some three thousand years ago, about the time of King David, the exuberant psalmist sang this hymn in praise of Yahweh, the creator of the visible universe. This song of the psalmist—and it was meant to be sung—proclaims God's power and provident care in his role as creator (vv. 3-10). His enthusiasm can be matched today as we sing that glorious anthem *How Great Thou Art!* Yahweh's providential concern in supplying the needs of wild animals, birds, creatures large and small, and of mankind points up the dependence of all creation on the generosity of God's hand. In verse 29, David describes what can happen if Yahweh does not maintain his providential care. The utter dependence of so many on their herds, or crops, and these in turn on sources of water, then as today in many parts of the world, helps us to appreciate the depth of gratitude expressed by God's people living on the fringes of the treacherous desert.

How beautiful the sentiment of the psalmist as he concludes his
ng in heartfelt gratitude:

> May the glory of the Lord endure forever;
>> may the Lord be glad in his works!
> He who looks upon the earth, and it trembles;
>> who touches the mountains, and they
>>> smoke!
> I will sing to the Lord all my life;
>> I will sing praise to my God while I live!
> Pleasing to him be my theme;
>> I will be glad in the Lord
> May sinners cease from the earth,
>> and may the wicked be no more.
> Bless the Lord, O my soul! Alleluia.

Day 7 of Week 1: Repetition
*Lord, show me again what Your gifts to me have been during this
week.*

During this last day of the first week of retreat it may be helpful
to return to one or more of the meditations which has proved especially meaningful to you—as long as it remains fruitful. Sometimes,
however, it is helpful to return to a meditation that was difficult or
not fruitful long enough to see if on this occasion it may become more
meaningful. Another approach is to use the examination of consciousness and review your experiences in prayer throughout the
week to date to discern the movement of spirits. That is, examine the
ways in which God, Our Father, is drawing you in the ways of Jesus,
and those ways in which the evil spirit may be attempting to undermine those efforts.

Time after time I came to your gate

Time after time I came to your gate
with raised hands, asking for more and yet more.

You gave and gave, now in
slow measure, now in sudden excess.

I took some, and some things I let
drop; some lay heavy on my hands;
some I made into playthings and broke
them when tired; till the wrecks and
the hoard of your gifts grew immense,
hiding you, and the ceaseless expectation
wore my heart out.

Take, oh take—has now become my cry.

Shatter all from this beggar's bowl;
put out this lamp of the importunate
watcher; hold my hands, raise me from
the still-gathering heap of your gifts
into the bare infinity of your uncrowded
presence.

RABINDRANATH TAGORE

Week 2: *The Principle and Foundation*

My attitude: Spiritual freedom is mine when I am seized so completely by the love of God that all the desires of my heart and all the actions, affections, thoughts and decisions which flow from them are directed to God, my Father, and his service and praise. My attitude is that of Samuel, "Here I am Lord, send me."

What I seek: I beseech you, Lord, to direct all my actions by your inspiration, to carry them on by your gracious help, that every prayer and work of mine may always begin from you and through you be happily ended.

Day 1 of Week 2: On Our Spiritual Freedom
The Foundation: Fact and Practice.

Because of the importance of this principle and foundation to our spiritual freedom, you the retreatant should read over the "foundation" a few times each week during Phase One of the retreat. These statements express the basic Christian formulation that responds to the young man in the Gospel, who asked Jesus "What must I do to have eternal life?" They are taken from Fleming's reading of the *Spiritual Exercises.*

God freely created us so that we might know, love, and serve him in this life and be happy with him forever. God's purpose in creating us is to draw forth from us a response of love and service here on earth, so that we may attain our goal of everlasting happiness with him in heaven.

All the things in this world are gifts of God, created for us, to be the means by which we can come to know him better, love him more surely, and serve him more faithfully.

As a result, we ought to appreciate and use these gifts of God insofar as they help us toward our goal of loving service and union with God. But insofar as any created things hinder our progress toward our goal, we ought to let them go.

In everyday life, then, we should keep ourselves indifferent or undecided in the face of all created gifts when we have an option and we do not have the clarity of what would be a better choice. We ought not to be led on by our natural likes and dislikes even in matters such as health or sickness, wealth or poverty, between living in the east or in the west, becoming an accountant or a lawyer.

Rather, our only desire and our one choice should be that option which better leads us to the goal for which God created us.

Day 2 of Week 2: Psalm 105: 1–45
"Recall the wondrous deeds that he has wrought ... for Israel!"

When praying this psalm or any other, a number of approaches may be used: (1) very slowly reading through the psalm, making its expression your own; or (2) letting certain lines or phrases capture your attention for the whole period—(see the Ignatian Second Method in our Introduction); or (3) meditatively reading through the psalm a number of times within the prayer period [258–60].

Focusing on God's faithfulness to mankind, this hymnic song recites Israel's history from Abraham to the Exodus and the conquest of the Promised Land. It is the story of God's hand providentially guiding and protecting his chosen people. This pentateuchal psalm summarizes the main points recorded in the first five books of the Bible. It is divided as follows: a call to worship—to "seek to serve him constantly" (vv. 1-6); Yahweh's covenant and gift of the land: "To you will I give the land of Canaan as your allotted inheritance" (vv. 7-11); his chosen people in Canaan (vv. 12-15); Joseph and Israel in Egypt (vv. 16-24) ; the plagues and exodus (vv. 28-34); Israel in the desert and coming into the Promised Land (vv. 39-44).

Reflect on your personal history from early life to the present. Are there events and turning points that you interpret as blessings and gifts, perhaps a sudden inspiration, a wave of unexpected strength arising from an unanticipated source that changed the course of your life in a beneficial way? Were you taken into slavery in your own "Egypt," and after a time in chains did God lead you through the parched desert back to the Promised Land?

Day 3 of Week 2: Awareness Meditation Practice
Feeling your body's sensations.

This awareness meditation practice can be carried out in many situations in part—for example, while waiting for an appointment, riding to or from work, etc. It will provide you with insight into how well or how poorly attuned your bodily senses are to registering sensations. As to many persons, it may come as a surprise to you how insensitive one can become, through tension and preoccupation. However, with the practice of awareness, you can "sensitize" your senses and become alive once again as they relax. The importance of this kind of meditation is that it dispels the nervous tension that is one of the biggest obstacles to dynamic concentration and to prayer. If you are relatively unaware of what your body is experiencing, how can you be attuned to spiritual movements within you? St. Ignatius referred to the importance of "discernment of spirits" so that delusions may disappear from your life. The awareness meditation practice will prepare you to discern more readily other movements within you, including the movement of spirits. And it will assist you greatly in preparing for the examination of consciousness.

Take up a posture that is comfortable and restful. Slowly read the following instructions, then close your eyes and become totally alive to the following sensations:

Now become aware of certain sensations in your body that you are feeling at this present moment, but of which you may commonly not be explicitly aware . . . Be aware of the touch of your clothes on your shoulders, on your back, or of your back touching the chair on which you sit. Now become aware of the feel of your hands as they touch each other or rest on your lap. Now be aware of your thighs or your buttocks pressing against your chair, of your feet touching your shoes, of your sitting posture. Repeat the sequence of awareness activities several times and attend to whether you experience new sensations as they are repeated.

It is important for you to "*feel*" the sensation of each part momentarily and then move on to another part of the body. End the exercise by opening your eyes gently. Reflect on those parts of your body in which you were aware of some sensation, noting whether it was barely perceptible, moderately so, or strongly felt. It may be surprising to realize how insensitive many parts of your body are to sensations. With repetition of the exercise you may gradually become more aware of subtle sensations. To that extent you become more fully alive. To a certain extent you prepare yourself as well to perceive, as an impartial observer, other interior movements that transcend the sensual experience.

This simple exercise produces a sense of relaxation in most people, a good preparation for prayer as it helps to dissipate nervous tension. When I first heard Tony de Mello speak about awareness meditation, I was, in the way of a university professor, suspicious of this approach—until its results were proven to me. Most of us are too little aware of the activity of our senses and as a result we live most of our lives either in the past or in the future but rarely in the present.

Reflect for some time about what parts of your life are lived in the past, regretting past mistakes, feeling guilty about past sins or failures, basking in the glow of past achievements, resenting past slights or injuries by other people. How much of your life is commonly devoted to the future? How much time do you spend, fearing possible setbacks, calamities, or unpleasantness, dreaming of future happiness, pleasure, or looking forward to future events? The only time that is real is the present moment and yet we so commonly discard the present experience as of trivial value in favor of the future or the past. The awareness meditation practice can change that and ourselves for the better, and free us so that we can pray *in the present*. From day to day keep track of whether you live more in the past, in the future or in the present. If you spend much time thinking in the present, you probably enjoy much peace of mind, and will find it so much easier to enter into prayer.

Day 4 of Week 2: Colossians 1: 3–20
"That you may be filled with the knowledge of his (Christ's) will . . . in whom we have redemption."

This Pauline message is divided: first, the beautiful and theologically rich thanksgiving (1:3-8) and prayer (1:9-14) for the Christians of the town of Colossae; and then the hymn extolling the pre-eminence of Christ, his person and his work (1:15-20).

Paul uses phrases that are practical expressions of faith, love and hope: "praying", "asking" (v. 9) and "giving thanks" to the Father for knowledge, wisdom, and understanding i.e. knowledge demands obedience to God's will (vv. 4-5). A traditional liturgical expression (vv. 12-13) refers in hymnic language to God's saving activity, expressing the belief that the Father has delivered us from the power of darkness. It is clear that salvation is already present, and that God has already brought us into the kingdom of his beloved Son.

Probably originating in the Judaic liturgy, the Christ hymn has the character of a primitive hymn of the early Church. Its theme is the role of Christ in creation, alluding to wisdom motifs in the Old Testament. Christ is praised as the image or icon of the invisible God, meaning that he shows forth God's presence in his person. As you prayerfully read from this passage of Scripture let your feelings of gratitude draw you to pray that you too "may be filled with the knowledge of his will through all spiritual wisdom and understanding to live in a manner worthy of the Lord. . .in whom we have redemption, the forgiveness of sins." Prayerfully recite or sing this hymn to the cosmic Christ, an attribute so loved by Teilhard de Chardin.

Day 5 of Week 2: Genesis 15: 1–21 & 22: 1–19
"Take your son Isaac, your only one, whom you love, and . . . offer him up as a holocaust."

Yahweh's promises to Abraham of a son and heir (15: 1-6) and a homeland (vv. 7-21) were accepted quite humanly by Abraham with a complaint and a somewhat skeptical request for a sign. In response to Yahweh's promise to Abraham that his descendants will be as numerous as the stars in the desert night sky, Abraham "put(s) his faith in the Lord," and wins Yahweh's favor. Then God tests Abraham in a most dramatic fashion, the tenth and greatest of his trials (22:1-19). Abraham proves himself absolutely trusting and obedient and without his earlier impassioned evasions. Having been thoroughly tested, he shows that he is a worthy founder of Israel.

This trial of Abraham and his response to God clarify the meaning in a concrete case of the application of the Principle and Foundation. As you are tested by trials that come into your life, remember that Abraham was only purified gradually by the testing but he reached the point that he could entrust his life and future unconditionally to God. In your meditation speak to God like Abraham and pray for the simplicity and sincerity required to respond authentically to God's calling of you.

Day 6 of Week 2: 1 Samuel 3: 1–21
"Speak, Lord, for your servant is listening."

This somewhat humorous and heartwarming passage has several layers of meaning, with at least two ready applications to this retreat. It begins with the observation that a revelation of the Lord was uncommon and visions infrequent. It ends with Samuel receiving frequent revelations at Shiloh. Eli and Samuel speak to each other twice and the Lord speaks to Samuel alone (vv. 10-14). Here, however, the Lord does not address Samuel's future but condemns Eli's house, indicating that there is no chance for expiation. Nevertheless, Eli accepts the judgment because "He is the Lord. He will do what he judges best" (v.18).

As you meditate upon this narrative which recounts the spontaneous, untutored generosity of the boy Samuel in training for the priesthood, reflect on the fact that he was unaware of how to discern the movement of spirits, another expression for "hearing the Lord call." At first Samuel thought that the call came from his mentor, who in fact was but a spiritually weak and blind companion whose "lamp of God" was nearly extinguished. Responding to Samuel's generous response, engage the Lord in prayer, asking that you too be given a generous, responsive heart, and pray for wisdom to learn the practice of Christian insight meditation or the fruitful practice of the consciousness examen.

Day 7 of Week 2: Repetition
"A review of the days thus far on this spiritual journey."

Return to those points that you have savored in a special way, and/or to phrases, ideas, or impulses that have challenged your sense of personal authenticity during the two weeks of this special spiritual journey that you are undertaking. Reflect especially, in a detached way, as if you were an interested spectator, on the interior movements, attractions or repulsions, so as to gain some insight into the the way that God, your Father, is drawing you to Him—speaking to you in the silence of your heart, as he did to Paul, to Abraham, to Samuel. They listened to the call of God, and struggled with their desires to be responsive, to be authentic persons. They felt as well the desire to be unburdened of the responsibilities of God's call, as each of us does.

Ignatius, in founding the Society of Jesus, used the principles of the Spiritual Exercises to establish a way of life for those who wished to be "contemplatives in action." The following excerpt from the Constitutions that Ignatius wrote, may be useful for your own concrete situation in life, as you set about in a more defined way to become a "contemplative in action." Although you may not be called to be a member of the formally established Society that Ignatius founded, you are being called to be companions of Jesus in a spirituality that can transform you and your world. God is offering you a covenant that promises that your spiritual progeny will be as numerous as the stars in the sky or the grains of sand on the seashore.

> For the preservation and development not only of the body or exterior of the Society but also of its spirit, and for the attainment of the objective it seeks, which is to aid souls to reach their ultimate and supernatural end, the means which unite the human instrument with God and so dispose it that it may be wielded dexterously by His divine hand are more effective than those which equip it in relation to men. Such means are, for example, goodness and virtue, and especially charity, and a pure intention of the divine service, and familiarity with God our Lord in spiritual exercises of devotion, and sincere zeal for souls for the sake of glory to Him who created and redeemed them and not for any other benefit. Thus it appears that care should be taken in general that all the members of the Society may devote themselves to the solid and perfect virtues and to spiritual pursuits, and attach greater importance to them than to learning and other natural and human gifts. For they are the interior gifts which make those exterior means effective toward the end which is sought (*Constitutions*, 813).

Meditating upon the wonderful ways in which God has entered your life to date, engage in prayerful thanksgiving with a grateful and joyous heart. Pray for true interior freedom—freedom to be called from your land of Haran to wherever God may summon you on your great adventure to become the father or mother of a great people.

Trust in God

The LORD is my light and my salvation;
    whom should I fear?
The LORD is my life's refuge;
    of whom should I be afraid?
When evildoers come at me
    to devour my flesh,
My foes and my enemies
    themselves stumble and fall.
Though an army encamp against me,
    my heart will not fear;
Though war be waged upon me,
    even then will I trust.

One thing I ask of the LORD;
    this I seek:
To dwell in the house of the LORD
    all the days of my life,
That I may gaze on the loveliness of the LORD
    and contemplate his temple.
For he will hid me in his abode
    in the day of trouble;
He will conceal me in the shelter of his tent,
    he will set me high upon a rock.
Even now my head is held high
    above my enemies on every side.
And I will offer in his tent
    sacrifices with shouts of gladness;
I will sing and chant praise to the LORD.

PSALM 27

Week 3: Sin and the Great Struggle

My attitude: What is it to be a Christian, a follower of Jesus? "It is to know that one is a sinner, yet called to be a companion of Jesus as Ignatius was. What is it to be a companion of Jesus today, to have values that tend to be in part cultural but in part counter-cultural? It is to engage, under the standard of the Cross, in the crucial struggle of our time: the struggle for faith and that struggle for justice which it includes." (Adapted from Decrees in the *Documents of the 32nd General Congregation of the Society of Jesus*, The Society's Response to the Challenges of our Age, Declaration: *Jesuits Today*, p. 7).

What I seek: Conscious of the high adventure, sublime destiny, and freedom for which I was created and of the vocation to which God invites me, I beg Him for a deep-felt understanding of my sin and of the disordered tendencies in my life that hobble me in my pursuit; that I may feel a need for change, and so turn to him for healing and forgiveness. I seek to rid myself of every form of greed and lust, of anger and resentment, and of delusion that I may rid myself of all that fetters me.

A Perspective on One's Progress in the "First Phase"

There is no deadline for you to acquire the ideas of the First Phase of the retreat. Let the dynamic of your prayer and God's interaction with you make them yours. Once you get deep enough into that kind of prayer you will be led by the Spirit into a "First Phase" experience.

For many people, sin refers to despicable acts performed or plotted by others. For many others, sin is an antiquated notion with no personal meaning. But for many people throughout the ages, sin and sinful tendencies are a fact of life, one aspect of being human. Throughout the ages, too, human beings aspiring to Spirit-inspired authenticity have sought forgiveness and have cried out for strength and a closer union with God.

Day 1 of Week 3: 2 Samuel 11: 1-12: 15
"You are the man!" "I have sinned against the Lord!"

One of the most dramatic stories of sin and repentance in the Bible is that of King David who lusted after Bathsheba, abducted her, had intercourse with her, made her pregnant, and arranged to have her husband, Uriah the Hittite, killed in battle. Nathan, the prophet, when he heard what the king had done, confronted him with the story of a rich man who stole the poor man's ewe. To that injustice David responded angrily in the poignant passage "As the Lord lives, the man who has done this merits death. He shall restore the ewe lamb fourfold because he has done this and has had no pity" (12:5-13). Then Nathan said to David: "You are the man!" David, having his sins revealed to him so dramatically, uttered that phrase of heart-felt repentance "I have sinned against the Lord." Nathan responded with that most welcome assurance: "The Lord on his part has forgiven your sin."

In meditating upon David's sins, including premeditated murder, we are faced with the chilling realization of the power of greed in the form of lust, even in the life of one of the greatest figures of the Old Testament, otherwise a hero and a man of God. In these respects David is like every man and every woman. Each of us is pulled in one direction by our sinfulness and drawn in the other direction to the loving embrace of God, our Father. Recognizing these two faces of human nature in yourself, let the Word of God speak to you, inspiring you to respond to God from a heart overflowing with many different emotions. Be mindful that the God who speaks to you in this Scripture passage is the God of David. From a heart that recognizes its frailty and at the same time hears the call, respond to love. Speak to the God of David—and to Jesus, Our Savior, who has redeemed us from our sins and from our sinfulness. And speak to the Holy Spirit, our source of wisdom and love. Beg of them what you seek at this time.

Day 2 of Week 3: Ignatius' First Exercise
Meditation on Three Sins and their consequences.

With my eyes fixed gratefully on the crucified Lord who saves me, I beg for the experience of "shame and confusion, as I consider the effects of even one sin as compared with my own sinful life. I may find it helpful to imagine myself as bound, helpless, alienated as I enter into these exercises dealing with sin" [47].

At this stage of the retreat, Ignatius becomes rather specific about both the preparation for, and the subject matter of our prayer. These instructions are to be found in the "First Exercise" [45 to 53] (see Fleming, pp. 33-37).

Fleming reads the PREPARATION for each of Ignatius' exercises of the First Phase of the retreat as follows: I always take a moment to call to mind the attitude of reverence with which I approach this privileged time with God. I recollect everything up to this moment of my day—my thoughts and words, what I have done and what has happened to me—and ask that God direct it all to his praise and service [46]."

The MEDITATION focuses on the effects of three sins: 1) the angels who rebelled against God [50]; 2) the sin of Adam and Eve [51]; and 3) the person who goes to hell [52]. As part of the COLLOQUY and related reflection [53] I ponder in the following way:

I look to myself—reflecting on how God creates because he loves and then becomes man out of love, and ultimately dies for my sins—and ask:

In the past, what response have I made to Christ?

How do I respond to Christ now?

What response should I make to Christ? As I look upon Jesus hanging upon the cross, I ponder whatever God may bring to my attention.

I close with an Our Father.

Day 3 of Week 3: Ignatius' Second Exercise
I, a sinner before a loving God and his gifts of creation!

PREPARATION: It is the same for this exercise as for the preceding exercise. Grateful to God who continues to save me up to this very minute, I ask for the Grace to experience "a growing and intense sorrow and even tears for my sins" [55]. The Setting is such that "I see myself as a sinner—bound, helpless, alienated—before a loving God and all his gifts of creation" [56]. "Without the detail of an examination of conscience, I let pass before my mind all my sins and sinful tendencies that permeate my life from my youth up to the very present moment. I let the weight of such evil, all stemming from me, be felt throughout my whole being" [57]. For a fuller amplification of the setting see [56-60].

COLLOQUY: How can I respond to a God so good to me in himself and who surrounds me with the goodness of his holy ones and all the gifts of his creation? All I can do is give thanks, wondering at his forgiving love, which continues to give me life up to this very moment. By his grace, I want to amend my life [61M].*

I close with an Our Father.

---

*One modification (M), in particular, that I believe Ignatius would have suggested, had the temper of his times permitted, is the inclusion of a colloquy to the Holy Spirit. Thus next, in Day 4 of Week 3, I refer to a fourfold colloquy instead of the triple colloquy detailed originally in the Third Exercise.

J.W.S.

Day 4 of Week 3: Ignatius' Third Exercise
A growing and intense sorrow for all my sins.

The PREPARATION and GRACE are the same as in the previous two exercises; in considering the SETTING I return to those thoughts and feelings that struck me most forcefully from those two exercises, reviewing those areas in which I experienced greater consolation or desolation, or greater spiritual appreciation. The purpose of the repetition is to let sink into my heart the movements of God through the already familiar subject matter [62].

In the presence of Mary, of Jesus her Son and of our Father in heaven, and of the Holy Spirit living within me, I beg for a deep knowledge and abhorrence of my sins, especially my complicity in the sins of the world against faith and against that justice which is integral to living faith.

In the midst of these considerations, a fourfold colloquy is suggested below, to show the intensity of my desire for God's gift of sorrow [63M].

COLLOQUY: First I go to Mary, our Mother, that she may ask, on my behalf, grace for three favors from her Son and Lord. These are: (1) A deep realization of what sin in my life is and a resulting abhorrence; (2) Some understanding of the disorder in my life due to sin; and (3) An insight into the world opposed to Christ that I may renounce it. Then I say a Hail Mary or a Memorare, or the like.

Next in the company of Mary, I ask the same petitions of her Son, that Jesus may obtain these graces from the Father for me. Then I say the "Soul of Christ" or some such prayer to Jesus. I then pray to the Holy Spirit living within me for wisdom and light. Then I say "Come Holy Spirit."

Finally I approach the Father, having been presented by both Jesus and Mary. Again I make the same requests of the Father, that he, the giver of all good gifts, may grant them to me. Then I close with an Our Father.

Day 5 of Week 3: Ignatius' Fourth Exercise
A return to what has been most meaningful!

REPETITION: This period of prayer is meant to be a repetition—sometimes called by Ignatius a Summary or a Résumé. The hope is that the mind becomes less active with ideas since the subject matter does not change, and as a result the heart is more central to the way I find myself responding. The prayer period itself will probably be less active but by the grace of God it may grow in intensity by praying once again in the manner of the four-fold COLLOQUY (to the persons of the Trinity and to Mary, the mother of Jesus [64M].

Day 6 of Week 3: Ignatius' Fifth Exercise
An experience of hell.

Confident of God's unfailing love for me and grateful that he continues to save me up to this very moment, I dare to allow wash over me and fill all my senses the morass of evil which I have been contemplating, that evil whose fullness and consequence is hell.

PREPARATION: It is the same as that in Days 2 through 5 of Week 3. The GRACE: I beg for a deep sense of the pain of loss which envelops the damned, so that if I were ever to lose sight of the loving goodness of God, at least the fear of such a condemnation will keep me from falling into sin [65]. The SETTING is an experience of hell [66,67,68, 69,70].

COLLOQUY: Once I have let the awfulness of this experience sink deep within me, I begin to talk to Christ our Lord about it. I talk to him about all the people who have lived—the many who lived before his coming and who deliberately closed in upon themselves and chose such a hell for all eternity, the many who walked with him in his own country and who rejected his call to love, the many who still keep rejecting the call to love and remain locked in their own chosen hell [71].

I give thanks to Jesus that he has not put an end to my life and allowed me to fall into any of these groups. All I can do is give thanks to him that up to this very moment he has shown himself to be loving and merciful to me. Then I close with an Our Father and/or the Soul of Christ.

Day 7 of Week 3: 1 John 1: 5–2: 6
"If we acknowledge our sins, he. . .will forgive our sins and cleanse us."

This letter, attributed by early Christian tradition to the beloved apostle, John, clarifies what it means to walk in light, what it means to walk in darkness or sin, and what can be done about it. To have fellowship with God (v.6) and with one another (v.7), we must walk in the light with the result that the blood of his Son, Jesus, cleanses us from all sin (v. 7). This cleansing requires a personal acknowledgement of our sin, following which he "will forgive our sins and cleanse us from every wrongdoing" (v.9).

John's stated purpose in writing is to keep Christians from sin (v. 2: 1). However, he recognizes that they may sin, but "we have an Advocate with the Father, Jesus Christ the righteous one," described as a sin-offering, "the Lamb of God" (1:29) "not for our sins only but for those of the whole world" (1 Jn 2: 2), thus revealing God's love.

In reflecting on our sinfulness, let us be grateful that we are called to walk in the way of Light, that we are called to live God's life even though, as human beings, we fall short of the goal. Let us acknowledge our sins and sinfulness with the assurance that Jesus will forgive us our sins and cleanse us from every wrongdoing. End the meditation period with the "Soul of Christ" or with the ancient prayer below.

God be in my head,
And in my understanding;
God be in mine eyes,
And in my looking;
God be in my mouth,
And in my speaking;
God be in my heart,
And in my thinking;
God be at my end and at my departing.

ANONYMOUS

An Hymn to God the Father

Wilt thou forgive that sin where I begun,
    Which is my sin, though it were done before?
Wilt thou forgive those sins through which I run,
    And do them still, though still I do deplore?
When thou hast done, thou hast not done,
        For I have more.

Wilt thou forgive that sin by which I won
    Others to sin? and made my sin their door?
Wilt thou forgive that sin which I did shun
    A year or two, but wallowed in a score?
When thou hast done, thou hast not done.
        For I have more

I have a sin of fear, that when I have spun
    My last thread, I shall perish on the shore;
Swear by thyself, that at my death thy Sun
    Shall shine as it shines now, and heretofore;
And, having done that, thou hast done,
        I have no more.

JOHN DONNE

Week 4: *A Sinner loved by God.*

My attitude: A thoughtful review of experience reveals that most of the ills of the world can be traced to personal greed, anger, hatred and delusion. These, in turn, lead us to treat ourselves and others in ways that are unbecoming of children of Our Divine Father, and of brothers and sisters of Jesus.

The gift I seek: In the presence of my Father in heaven, Jesus, my brother and companion, and the Holy Spirit, my consolation and strength, I ask for the gift of experiencing myself as a loved sinner, but to know my sinfulness and to purify my mind so well that I may experience a growing desire for conversion, a new insight into the tactics of God's enemy, and a renewed enthusiasm to follow Jesus.

A Reflection on Sin versus Peace and Justice

Today, perhaps more so than at any period in history, we are aware of widespread injustice in vastly different forms in many parts of the world and in various segments of society. In the decrees of the 32nd General Congregation of the Society of Jesus, the declaration "*Jesuits Today,*" expresses a point of view that could well be adopted by all of us as we seek to promote peace and justice in a setting of faith. The sections below summarize three particularly important reflections:

16. (A,6): Ignorance of the Gospel on the part of some, and rejection of it by others, are intimately related to the many grave injustices prevalent in the world today. Yet it is in the light of the Gospel that men will most clearly see that injustice springs from sin, personal and collective, and that it is made all the more oppressive by being built into economic, social, political, and cultural institutions of worldwide scope and overwhelming power.

17. (A,7) Conversely, the prevalence of injustice in a world where the very survival of the human race depends on men caring for and sharing with one another is one of the principal obstacles to belief: belief in a God who is justice because he is love.

36. (E,26) Coming from many different countries, cultures, and social backgrounds, but banded together in this way, we try to focus all our efforts on the common task of radiating faith and witnessing to justice. We are deeply conscious of how often and how grievously we ourselves have sinned against the Gospel; yet it remains our ambition to proclaim it worthily: that is, in love, in poverty, and in humility.

Day 1 of Week 4: Psalm 103: 1–22
Remember all his kindnesses in forgiving all our offenses!

Reflect that the Book of Psalms is regarded highly, not only as a religious document, but also as the songbook of the Church. The Psalter is not just a lyrical record of venerable religious tradition of ages that have passed away, but it is also a most moving and grace-filled link with the God and the people of God of the Old Testament.

In the devout recitation or singing of this hymn of praise, Psalm 103, as well as Psalms 104 and 105 (Day 6 of Week 1 and Day 2 of Week 2 respectively), we return to our spiritual roots in Israel in the 10th century B.C.—around the time of King David. Psalm 103 is also a hymn of thanksgiving in which the specific reason for such gratitude is that the singer's sins are forgiven. The introduction sets the tone of praise and thanksgiving and the body of the psalm expresses the many reasons for praise and gratitude. It concludes as it begins with the echo-like phrase, "Bless the Lord, O my soul!"

With a heart filled with gratitude for God's unconditional love and mindful of your sinfulness let the individual words and phrases of the Word of God speak to you, and speak in turn to God, your Father, to his Son, and to the Holy Spirit from the fullness of your heart. Pray also to Mary, the Mother of Jesus, and your mother as well, because you are members of his mystical Body.

Day 2 of Week 4: Practice of CIM
Toward a deeper sensitivity to my body sensations and my emotions.

This exercise is a deepening of the one in Day 3 of Week 1, and it is concerned with body sensations and experience of emotions. More specifically, however, this Christian Insight Meditation or CIM is designed to help you recognize sensations where before you may have felt none. It is a matter of developing greater sensitivity to what goes on in your body and mind, but it will require that you put up with your boredom. You must be prepared to practice these exercises over a long period of time, confident that the lack of novelty will be compensated by increased depth of sensitivity.

Take a comfortable position, one that you can maintain for five to ten minutes without moving. Close your eyes and repeat the Day 3 exercise mentioned above, moving from the top of your head to your toes and noting where you are most sensitive to sensations and also those areas where you experience little or no sensation. If your mind wanders, bring it patiently back to the exercise as soon as you become aware of the wandering.

Now choose just one small area where you have little or no sensation and focus on it endeavoring to recognize every sensation there, as for example your knee or your face. Even if at first the area seems completely devoid of sensation, do not give up but return to the previous exercise for a while. Then try that area again until you notice some sensation there, no matter how faint. Once you notice some sensation, stay with it. Note what kind of sensation it is, such as itching, pain, burning, tightness, twitching, throbbing, numbness, or more pleasant feelings of relaxation, strength, exhilaration.

The Buddhist meditation practice of sitting motionless for long periods of time has the effect that after a time, discomfort gives way to faint pain in one's knees or sitting bones or the like. This pain may increase until it becomes very strong, may make you sweat, and may require you to change position. In addition to noting the bodily sensations that develop or change their location and intensity, your emotions should be observed. As discomfort arises and increases, you may become aware that emotions that lie below the surface of your consciousness begin to surface, and gradually or suddenly flare up in intensity. For example, you may identify emotions of anger directed toward some individual or situation; emotions related to greed in any one of its several forms. These might be sexual fantasies or delusions, or fantasies of exaggerated desires for praise or honors, and the like.

After carrying out each part of the exercise for some extended period of time, depending on your proficiency and endurance (say, 5 to 30 minutes), reflect on whether you have become more aware of bodily sensations. Reflect, also, on what emotions you are able to identify—both base emotions such as anger, and those that are more lofty, such as contentment, benevolence, and the like. As you become accustomed to this kind of practice, you will discover peace and exhilaration not unlike that which you experience when you watch the waves of the sea breaking on a shore, or when you witness a beautiful sunset.

Centering Prayer for Peace and Stillness

I suggest that you begin each period of prayer with this exercise. Keep at it until you find peace and stillness that is found in centering prayer, and then move on to whatever form of prayer you prefer to practice. End this awareness meditation in a colloquy with the Holy Spirit asking for the insight to recognize the subtle physical and emotional movements that are yours, insight into those gentle interior movements by which your heavenly Father draws you to himself, as well as to those movements that take place in the baser side and which pull you away from the path of Jesus' love.

Day 3 of Week 4: Matthew 13: 1–23
"Many prophets and righteous people longed to see what you see but did not!"

Picture yourself as having been selected by Jesus, as indeed you have been, to travel with him and learn the lessons that he teaches to you and the other disciples as well as to the crowds of people that turn up wherever he goes. "Jesus went out of the house and sat down by the sea. Such great crowds gathered around him that he got into a boat and sat down, and the whole crowd stood along the shore. And he spoke to them at length in parables" (Mt 13: 1-3).

Linger upon each word and phrase of Jesus, and of his other disciples, as in this discourse and discussions that followed. How elated and humbled you feel to hear the words: "knowledge of the mysteries of the kingdom of heaven has been granted to you" (Mt 13: 11). Out of the fullness of your heart speak to Jesus, and express your gratitude for calling you to this great adventure that involves the coming of his kingdom.

Day 4 of Week 4: Luke 15: 1–10
The Parables of the Lost Sheep and the Lost Coin

All the parables in this chapter are united by the theme of joy over the recovery of what was lost, and Jesus tells us emphatically that the parables apply to the return of the repentant sinner. This statement was far from being out of character for Jesus, who was looked down upon because he was a friend of tax collectors and sinners, and as such was the subject of snide comment by the Scribes and Pharisees (see Lk 15: 1 and 7: 39).

The shepherd's joy is like God's joy. His love for the individual sheep, carrying it back on his shoulders to the flock with great joy, is like God's love. Note that he did not drive the wandering sheep back to the fold with a whip and in a rage. The joy that reigns in heaven, that Jesus refers to, is over the change of heart (*metanoia* see Lk 3:3 and 5:32) of the sinner. Speak to Jesus in this extravagant, contemplative spirit and pray for repentance and, what may be more difficult, the realization of the great love that Jesus has for the sinner, especially when that sinner may be you.

After experiencing the reality of sin as alienation, your own helplessness to do anything about it, perhaps the inability to believe in the love of God for you or your world, you may feel drawn to open yourself to the healing love of God. How happy you should be to *experience* yourself to be a loved sinner. This experience of salvation may stir up in you a strong desire to share with others the "good news," to be a follower and companion of Jesus.

Day 5 of Week 4: A Fantasy Exercise
How precious my life.

Now you, the retreatant, will exercise your imaginative faculty by creating a series of mental images about a profound, personal experience:

Imagine that you are going to the doctor to find out the results of tests that have been taken on you. The doctor is going to give them to you today. The tests could reveal some serious illness. Notice what you are feeling while you are on your way to the doctor's office...

You are now in his waiting room...Notice all the details of the room...the color of the walls, the prints on it...the furniture...the reviews and magazines there...Is there anyone else waiting for the doctor?...If there is, take a good look at the other person or persons in the room, their features, their clothes...Notice what you are feeling while you wait to be called into the office...

You are called in now...Take a look at the doctor's office...notice all the details, the furniture...Is the room bright or dim?...Take a good look at the doctor, his features, the way he is dressed...What kind of person is he?...

He begins to talk to you and you notice he seems to be hiding something from you...You tell him to speak to you quite openly... Then, with much compassion in his eyes, he tells you that the tests show that you have a disease that is incurable...You ask him how much longer you have to live...He says, "Two months of active life at the most...then a month or two in bed."

What is your response to this news?...What do you feel?...Stay for a while with those feelings...Now walk out of the doctor's office and into the street...Continue to stay with your feelings...Look at the street: is it crowded or empty?...Notice the weather: is the day bright or cloudy?...

Where are you going?...Do you feel like talking with anyone?...With whom?...

You eventually get back to your home and you share your new-found secret with your loved one(s) or close friend. What do you say to express what is in your heart? Your friend asks you what you want to do in the two months of active life you have. What do you choose to do?...How do you plan to spend those two months?...

You are at work with your colleagues...Do they know about you?...What are you feeling in their company?...

Go to your room now and write a letter to your supervisor or the one to whom you report, explaining the situation and asking to be eventually relieved of your work...What do you say in the letter?...Compose it in your mind right now...

It is late at night now and you are able to enjoy a weekend in a retreat house...Everyone else has gone to bed...You make your way into the chapel where it is completely dark except for the soft glow of the sanctuary lamp. . .You sit down and gaze at the tabernacle. . .Look at Jesus for a while. . .What do you say to him?. . .What does he say to you?. . .What are you feeling?. . . (de Mello, pp. 83-84).

One of the things most people gain from this exercise is an intense appreciation of and love for life. Many are surprised to find that they do not fear death as much as they thought they would.

Too frequently it is only when we lose something that we appreciate it and are grateful for it. No one values health so much as one who is sick. But why do we have to wait till we lose sight, health, or friends before we appreciate them and enjoy them?

As the days and weeks of the allotted two months draw to a close. . .how do I feel not just about my illness but about my sinfulness? Remember the parables of the lost sheep and the lost coin, and the Prodigal Father? Do I feel trusting enough in Jesus to believe that he will put me on his shoulders and carry me to his flock? I pray that I may experience repentance. If it were today, what would my unfinished business be? What would Jesus say to me at my judgment?

Day 6 of Week 4: Luke 15: 11–32
The Parable of the Prodigal Father.

This most famous of Jesus' parables, a literary masterpiece, traditionally misnamed "the parable of the prodigal son," provides spiritual insight into the profound, generous, and almost unbelievable acceptance that characterizes the kingdom of God. The story pivots on the father's prodigal love for his two sons. Under Jewish law, the first son received a double share of the inheritance (Dt 21: 17); the younger son a third, but normally the division of property took place at the father's death. The younger son in this story, in demanding his share, cuts his family ties and takes everything, with no intention of coming back. His departure with a large share of the estate implies a loss to both the father and the older brother, thus fueling the latter's animosity.

In meditating, try to expand on the details of the story from your own first- or second-hand experience. The father's only concern is that his son has returned, that he is alive and wants to be back.

As we meditate on this story of the adventuresome, wayward son, and his faithful, steady, hard-working brother, and their father who loved both, but in different ways, let us respond with the joy that Jesus must feel at the return of every son and daughter of his father. Let us respond to the father's heartfelt demand, "now we must celebrate and rejoice, because your brother was dead and has come to life again; he was lost and has been found." How can we doubt the reality of God's love for the sinner, the God who looks to the horizon day and night longing for the sight of his beloved son returning home.

Day 7 of Week 4: Application of the Senses
"Your father has slaughtered the fattened calf because he has [your brother] back safe and sound."

This is a special kind of repetition. One of the refreshing ways of going back to the well of meditation and contemplation with enjoyment and fruit is to make use of the full range of application of the senses to scenes that you have visited before. For instance, you may explore the meditation of the Prodigal Father more fully in this way. Additionally, new dimensions may emerge as you explore whether you are more like the father, or the elder, or the younger brother. Thus you put yourself into the story. Are there elements of all three people in you? What do you need to do for your attitude to become more like that of the father? If you recognize some resentment in yourself, or some hatred that needs to be healed, it may be helpful to return to this meditation as an awareness meditation such as that in Day 3 of Week 2.

This kind of exercise, as Ignatius has observed, is "making the history present," and, therefore, does not so much concern the past as the graced reality of the present. This effort to become present to Jesus in a particular mystery, requires the imaginative senses: "to see the persons" [106], usually the first way that we humans get to know another; "to hear what the persons say" [107], another natural way of coming to know someone better; and "to observe what the persons are doing" [108]. All of these sense perceptions are ways in which a personal relationship can be fostered. As you feel moved to contemplation you may feel drawn to engage in the fourfold colloquy

COLLOQUY: This is a prayerful, reverent conversation for which we can prepare "by thinking out what I ought to say to the three divine Persons, or to the eternal Word Incarnate, or to his mother, Our Lady, begging—according to the degree to which I am moved in my affectivity—better to follow and imitate our Lord, thus *becoming a renewed person*. Then conclude by saying the Our Father" [109M]. Stanley sums up this method: "it is through the motions of my own affectivity that the mystery happens to me, that I am brought to be present to Jesus. A very ancient Christian document by an anonymous writer speaks of the risen Christ as 'the One who appears as new, is discovered to be from of old, is daily born anew in the hearts of believers'" (p. 87).

Discipline

Throw away thy rod,
Throw away thy wrath:
    O my God,
Take the gentle path.

For my heart's desire
Unto thine is bent:
    I aspire
To a full consent.

Not a word or look
I affect to own,
    But by book
And thy book alone.

Though I fail, I weep;
Though I halt in pace,
    Yet I creep
To the throne of grace.

Then let wrath remove;
Love will do the deed;
    For with love
Stony hearts will bleed.

Love is swift of foot,
Love's a man of war,
    And can shoot,
And can hit from far.

Who can 'scape his bow?
That which wrought on thee,
    Brought thee low,
Needs must work on me.

Throw away thy rod:
Though man frailties hath,
    Thou art God:
Throw away thy wrath.

GEORGE HERBERT

TRANSITION FROM PHASE ONE TO PHASE TWO

A Consideration or Appeal to Reason

St. Ignatius presents this exercise, entitled Del Rey, "About the King" [91-98], not as a contemplation but as a CONSIDERATION calculated to lead to contemplation. By CONSIDERATION Ignatius means an appeal to reason rather than an appeal to the heart as in contemplation, by which, as we noted in our section, "Some Ignatian Forms of Prayer," the devout heart is raised to Jesus through consolation. This exercise has long been referred to as "The Kingdom," but this term is not used in the Ignatian text, a careful reading of which reveals that this exercise is concerned mainly with the challenging call by the risen Jesus to follow him.

In the month-long Ignatian retreat [20] there is a recommended reduction in formal prayer periods during this "break day." St. Ignatius seems to have looked upon the exercise, here named "The Call of Christ the Eternal King," as a transition from Phase One to Phase Two. As such it represents a milestone in the retreat process. In adapting this guideline to the Nineteenth Annotation or ISEL retreat, one should give at least several days and possibly all of Week 5 to it. The exercise should be considered in formal prayer twice during the week. The rest of the week is free of set prayer periods and, as a result, is somewhat informal. It should, nevertheless, be prayerfully relaxed.

A Perspective on the Call of Christ to Each of Us

Ignatius nowhere in the First Phase develops a meditation that focuses specifically on the mercy of Jesus, but he concretizes the mercy of God in the exercise entitled "Christ the King and His Call" [*Spiritual Exercises*, Guidelines 91-98].

There is a way of showing love by doing something for another person, as a father can send his child gifts while living far away. But a far greater sign of love is shown by being present and mutually involved, such as a father spending time with his child. . . . It is in this second way that Ignatius presents the parable of a king calling to all the inhabitants of his kingdom. . . .

The parable (of the Prodigal Son) is intended to be a pale image— though it has been repeated many times in actual human history—of the call which Jesus Christ gives to each person. He not only identifies himself as our personal savior but invites each man, woman, and child to be involved with him in working for the salvation of their fellow men and women and their world. The victory has been won in Christ, though it is still in process in us and in our world.

Ignatius would have us understand even more deeply the mercy of God as it is extended by the very means of this call to work with Christ and to follow him in all the ways that our devotion to him can draw us. Ignatius proposes that we consider the response which a very generous person would make to Jesus, but he very carefully does not demand that we make the same response [97-98]. In fact, no colloquy is outlined, though a grace has been sought in terms of hearing and responding to the Call of Christ [91].

This exercise—put together by Ignatius to introduce us to the present and risen Christ and to his call—is best described as a "consideration." In a consideration the mind is absorbed with the search for truth, rather than a meditation on it. St. Bernard defines a consideration as "a true and certain insight of the mind concerning any reality, or a grasp of the truth that is free of all doubt." This consideration is meant to be an aid to contemplation [91]. "The evident logic involved in a consideration does not demand the kind of reasoning process which the meditation form does. Both prayer forms, however, ultimately call for some response from us. . . .

The "Foundation of the Second Phase"

Often commentators identify the call of Christ as the "Foundation of the Second Phase." As Ignatius gives the directions for this period, he indicates that this exercise should be gone through twice [99]. The common practice of the repose "period or break period between the Phases" of the Exercises apparently drew its inspiration from the relaxation from the seven exercises per week in the First Phase to the two exercises during the several days in the Kingdom. . . .

Although there are only the two exercises in this period, with the same material about the Kingdom repeated twice, the period itself is a most important one for the dynamic of the retreat. The Call of Christ is meant to rouse in the retreatant not only a generous response of gratitude but the commitment to the person of Jesus and to his work. The Kingdom exercise, then, acts as a bridge between the gratitude for the mercy of God seen in Christ in the First Phase and the study of his person and his work in the succeeding Phases. The Kingdom exercise at the same time is an encounter with Jesus as he is now—our risen Savior—who continues to invite each one of us to be his apostle for our own time and place. (Adapted from Fleming, 1973, *The Ignatian Spiritual Exercises*, "Understanding a Dynamic," pp. 9-11).

Modern Difficulties with the Concept of "King"

Many of us today are not as spontaneously responsive to the concept of being led into battle by a king as were Ignatius and others in the past. Even Teilhard de Chardin, who is very responsive to the Cosmic Christ as the King of the Universe and the Omega toward which all creation moves as to its goal, uses other images. Teilhard prefers a term from nature, the "Body," a favorite image drawn from St. Paul. Following St. Teresa's image of our role, we are Christ's hands ministering to the needs of the world, since "He has no hands but yours." We and other members of Christ's mystical body are his feet, his eyes, and his ears as we minister to His world and participate in the creation of the Noosphere and in bringing the universe to completion under Christ's Kingship. For other problems with the language of this CONSIDERATION, see Stanley (pp. 70–72)

It is clear that the call to join the risen Lord in his undertaking of redemption within the Church is issued to all human beings without exception. Hugo Rahner makes the important point that "the immediate purpose is not the formation of an apostolic vocation, but the realization that the Kingdom can ultimately be established by people who offer themselves unreservedly to Christ the King. . . .carnal and worldly love are only the immediate objects to be fought against; the real battle is against the enemy of human nature, and the victory was, and always will be, possible only through the cross" (*Ignatius the Theologian*, pp. 110-11).

The preliminaries for Phase Two of the Exercises begin where both Mark and John start their narratives of Jesus' public ministry with the call to his disciples to follow him (Mk 1: 16-20; Jn 1: 35-51), the one whom Philip recognized as the one "about whom Moses wrote in the law, and also the prophets, Jesus son of Joseph, from Nazareth (Jn 1: 45)."

Christ's Life: the Basic Theological Principle

As we begin to look closely at the life, works, and mission of Jesus Christ, let us recall Hugo Rahner's observation on the Ignatian manner of contemplating the life of our Lord: "Ignatius' principal concern could be summed up as bringing to mind the life of Christ, with particular reference to the cross" (p. 99). "Thus for Ignatius the life of Christ is the basic theological principle behind all Christian spiritual life—ultimately nothing more or less than the conforming of one's entire being through grace with the crucified and risen Lord of glory."

Week 5: The Call and the Coming of the Eternal King

My attitude: Although spoken by Pope John Paul II to the Jesuits of the 33rd General Congregation of the Society on September 2, 1983, these words are equally applicable to all Christians today: "Your vocation consists precisely in seeking to follow Christ, Redeemer of the world, by being his collaborators in the redemption of the entire world; consequently you should excel in the service of the Divine King, as stated in the offering that concludes the Contemplation on the Kingdom of Christ in the *Spiritual Exercises* of Saint Ignatius." Recall also that in its final document the Congregation declared: "Our religious life has been enriched by the opportunity to 'labor with' Jesus in the greater service of the Kingdom (34)." What our Holy Father proposes for Jesuits is no less a statement of the vocation of the lay companions of Jesus. The King's call is to high adventure, an invitation to companionship, to experience his loving care and to join with him in the service of His people. This is a call issued to every generous Christian who seeks to help our Saviour to fulfill his mission on earth.

The gift I seek: I ask the Lord for this gift: that I may be able to hear Jesus the King when he calls and that I may be ready and willing to do what he asks. I beg further for the gift of companionship with Jesus such that my awareness of him will become more profound, my experience of his love will become more intense, my union with his saving mission will be daily more intimate.

Consideration 1 for Week 5: The Exercises [91–98]
Christ the Eternal King and His Call.

Basically these exercises of Week 5 build on the Principle and Foundation of Week 2 (refer to [23]), where Ignatius stresses the necessity of being poised in a state of emotional equilibrium (which is what Ignatius meant by "indifference") before all creatures. These meditations on the call and coming of Jesus Christ, the King, are a call to complete generosity, to a seeking of the "better choice."

PREPARATION: As always, it is to place myself before God in reverence and to beg him to direct everything in my day more and more to his service and praise [91]. The GIFT I SEEK: I ask of our Lord that I might be able to hear his call, and that I might be ready and willing to do what he wants.

THE SETTING consists of two parts, the first naturally leading to the more important second part:

1. First, I "put myself in a mythical situation—the kind of story-truth of which fairy tales are made. I imagine a human leader, selected and raised up by God our Lord himself; every man, woman,

and child of good will is drawn to listen to such a leader and is inspired to follow the call" [92]. The leader's address to all men and women rings out in words like these: "I want to overcome all diseases, all poverty, all ignorance, all oppression and slavery—in short, all the enemies of mankind. Whoever works with me will share in the victory with me." How could anyone not want to be a part of so challenging and noble an adventure? [93-94M]

2. In the second part, I consider Jesus Christ our Lord and his call. If a human leader can have such an appeal to us, how much greater is the attraction of the God-Man, Jesus Christ, our Leader and King. . . .he specially calls each person in a particular way with the appeal: "It is my will to win over the whole world, to conquer sin, hatred, and death—all the enemies between mankind and God. Whoever wishes to join me in this mission must be willing to labor with me, so that by following me in suffering, he may follow me in glory" [95].

With God inviting and with victory assured, how can anyone of right mind not give himself over to Jesus and his work? [96].

Persons who are of great heart and are set on fire with zeal to follow Jesus Christ, eternal King and Lord of all, will not only offer themselves entirely for such a mission, but will act against anything that would make their response less total. They would want to express themselves in some such words as these: [97].

Eternal Lord and King of all creation, humbly I come before you. Knowing the support of Mary, your mother, and all your saints, I am moved by your grace to offer myself to you and to your work. I deeply desire to be with you in accepting all wrongs and all abuse and all poverty, both actual and spiritual—and I deliberately chose this, if it is for your greater service and praise. If you, my Lord and King, would so call and choose me, then take and receive me into such a way of life. [98]

COLLOQUY: If you are moved by his grace to do so, speak to Jesus, the eternal Lord and King of all creation, and offer yourself to him and to his work, even deeply desiring to be with him in accepting all wrongs and all abuse and all poverty, both actual and spiritual, if it is for his greater service and praise.

Consideration 2 for Week 5: Colossians 1: 15–23
The King of the Universe calls me personally.

The pre-eminence of Christ in his person and his work is the subject of Paul's impassioned and expansive view of Christ that Paul presented to the Colossians. It is an all encompassing portrayal of the great adventure of the universe and the individual persons placed in it: "in him were created all things in heaven and on earth, the visible and invisible. . . .and you. . . .he has now reconciled. . .through his death, to present you. . .before him" (v. 16, 21). This is also the magnificent view of the universe and of our role in helping to re-create the Kingdom of God that so inspired Teilhard de Chardin.

The following contemporary ideas adapted from Teilhard build quite naturally from what the Apostle Paul portrayed so beautifully as Christ's universe:

1. Gratitude that I should have the opportunity given me to participate in shaping the Universe. The probability of my coming into existence accidentally as the person that I am is small.

2. My prehistory goes back to 15 to 20 billion years ago and my makeup—biologically, chemically, psychically, etc.—is very complex, with my ancestry traced ultimately back to the Universe (15 to 20 billion years old) through the Earth's 5 billion year old history.

3. I have a limited span of years on Earth to collaborate with God in creating the Earth and the Universe, to build up the Noosphere with all the many products of my mind and heart.

4. The Earth and the Universe are alive and are becoming "Christ" through mankind's active collaboration as expressed by Teilhard.

5. When the transformation is complete, Christ will be fully recognizable as King of the Universe in the fullness of that title.

Teilhard de Chardin expresses beautifully the kingship of the Cosmic Christ in the chapter, "Communion with God through Earth," (*Writings in Time of War*, pp.57-58):

> By grace, Jesus Christ is united to all sanctified souls, and since the bonds that link souls to him in one single hallowed mass end in him and meet in him, and hold together by him, it is he who reigns and he who lives; the whole body is His in its entirety. . . .through his Incarnation he entered not only into mankind but also into the universe that bears mankind. . . .with the dignity and function of the directive principle, of centre upon which every form of love and every affinity converge. Christ has a *cosmic body* that extends throughout the whole universe. . . .
>
> The Incarnation is a making new, a restoration, of all the universe's forces and powers; Christ is the Instrument, the Centre, the End, of the *whole* of animate and material creation; through him, everything is created, sanctified, and vivified. This is the. . .teaching of St. John and St. Paul (that most 'cosmic' of all sacred writers) and it has passed into the most solemn formulas of the Liturgy. . .without ever being able to grasp or appreciate its profound and mysterious significance, bound up as it is with understanding of the universe. . . .By the Incarnation, which redeemed man, the very Becoming of the Universe, too, has been transformed. Christ is the term of even the natural evolution of living things; evolution is holy.

Lord, make me bold as St. Paul and St. John so that I may understand, as Teilhard de Chardin did, the vast scope of Our Savior's plan for all the universe's forces and powers. In conclusion, I can place myself among the Colossians in ancient Phrygia who were reminded with poetic forcefulness of who and what Christ is to each of us (1:15–20):

The Preeminence of Christ
His Person and Work

He is the image of the invisible God,
    the firstborn of all creation
For in him were created all things in heaven
        and on earth,
    the visible and the invisible,
    whether thrones or dominions or
        principalities or powers;
    all things were created through him and for
        him.
He is before all things,
and in him all things hold together.
He is the head of the body, the church.
He is the beginning, the firstborn from the
        dead,
    that in all things he himself might be
        preeminent.
For in him all the fullness was pleased to
        dwell,
    and through him to reconcile all things
        for him,
making peace by the blood of his cross
[through him], whether those on earth or
        those in heaven.

PREPARATION FOR PHASE TWO PRAYER

Contemplation of the Life of Christ

The following description of the experience of Phase Two is adapted from "The Experience of the First and Second Weeks of the Spiritual Exercises," an important study by William A. Barry, S.J. (pp. 100-101):

> The retreatant who has had a deep "Phase One experience" commonly enters the contemplation of the life of Christ with enthusiasm and gratitude. Contemplation of Jesus, being something brand new, may prove to be enjoyable, and relatively easy. One retreatant said: "There doesn't seem to be enough time in the day." Prayer periods seem to go by in a flash.
>
> In the initial enthusiasm the retreatant may concentrate on Jesus' kindness and sympathy, his care for the sick and suffering, his anti-legalism, his comfortable relation with the Father and his desire to bring others into that relationship. She may be captivated by the positive aspects of being with him, of answering yes to his "Come, follow me."
>
> It may happen, however, that you, the retreatant, may not advert to or take seriously, for example, the opposition Jesus encounters, even though this is explicitly presented. If so this probably means that you are praying out of your strength. After a few weeks the novelty may wear off; the prayer may become less enthralling; boredom can set in as it appears that Jesus just repeats cures and the same message. If this happens you will have to attend more carefully to elements in the life of Christ and in your prayer that will be more difficult. Then you may be praying out of your weakness or even out of your desolation.
>
> If that happens you may find that this "doldrum" period is a prelude to another conversion experience which I liken to the "Phase One experience" already described. Indeed, we venture the hypothesis that the "doldrums" are a form of resistance to entering this experience, that somehow or other you, the retreatant, are becoming aware of "the cost of discipleship" and may be resisting without even knowing it.

The Contemplative Prayer of Phase Two

Additional insights into the contemplative prayer of Phase Two are provided below. They are adapted by Fleming from Barry's 1973 article on the internal dynamic of these weeks of the Exercises (1983, pp. 9-11):

Ignatius opens up Phase Two proper with about three weeks of exercises on the incarnation, birth, and hidden life of Jesus. The structure of each week is similar to the week described in Phase One, with new matter being presented in both the first and second exercise period, followed by repetitions, with the final exercise being identified as an application of senses. . . .

The grace sought (expressed in the third preludes) and the colloquy, again give us the sense of direction or movement according to the phase of the retreat. The grace consistently desired is "to know Jesus more intimately so that I can love him more and follow him more closely." The colloquies tend to sharpen up the desire according to the particular mystery of Christ's life which has provided the matter for prayer. . . .

The way of praying found in Phase Two and in the succeeding phases most clearly bears the special mark of Ignatius' insight. Ignatius describes this kind of prayer as *contemplation* (see Introduction) and he gives to it his own special traits. His style of contemplation takes for its content various incidents (which are also called mysteries in Christian tradition) of the life of Christ as depicted in the gospels. Every incident recounted in scripture by the evangelist is potential matter for this kind of praying. . . .

It is by means of this style of contemplative prayer that Ignatius has discovered a way for the retreatant to imbibe Jesus' attitudes and approaches to God, to men and women, and to his world. The more we enter into gospel contemplation, the more we heighten the connaturality of our own way of living with the way that Christ lives. By the grace we seek and by the prayer-method we use, we find ourselves drinking in the experiences of Jesus, so that we begin to assimilate his values, his loves, his freedom. This style of praying provides the necessary context of decision-making or discernment which forms an essential part of Phase Two and is meant to be an abiding part of a Christian's life that is shaped by the Exercises.

Further Directions by Ignatius from the Exercises

In these guidelines Ignatius is particularly concerned with deepening the contemplations during Phase Two by a singleminded concentration on the subject matter of the specific week under consideration [127], and by observing in some systematic way the order of the prayer time so as to lay the basis for a life of prayer [128]. Prudence is called for in adapting the number of prayer periods to one's age, health or other factors [129], and in using the aids for prayer. For example, on awakening remember your desire to grow in intimate knowledge of Jesus in order to love and serve him better. Similarly it will be helpful to recall at various times in the day the particular event from Our Lord's life that you are contemplating. The use of many other helps such as darkness and light, penance, and other aids for prayer, all of which aim at the good progress of the retreat are suggested in Guideline [130].

Remember also that as we come to know Jesus more intimately and love him more ardently during Phase Two we will come to know and love the Holy Spirit as well. They are inseparable. Listen to Paul as the Romans listened: "If the Spirit of the one who raised Jesus from the dead dwells in you, the one who raised Christ from the dead will give life to your mortal bodies also, through his Spirit that dwells in you (v.11)."

Keep listening. Paul repeats and repeats to remind us of our destiny of glory when he says "that the sufferings of this present time are as nothing compared with the glory to be revealed for us (v.18). . . .And the one who searches hearts knows what is the intention of the Spirit, because it intercedes for the holy ones according to God's will (v.27)."

Finally Ignatius is concerned with safeguards for preparing for prayer periods so as to maximize their impact [131].

Additional guidelines suitable especially for Phase Two may also be found later in the *Exercises*. The guidelines are also meant to be helpful in understanding the interior movements, especially consolation and spurious consolation, which are a part of our spiritual lives [328-336]. These guidelines are more subtle than the norms described in Phase One because commonly in the progress of a good person's life the direction of all movements appears to be towards God.

I sing of a maiden
     That is makeles;
King of all kings
     To her son she ches.

He came all so still
     There his mother was,
As dew in April
     That falleth on the grass.

He came all so still
     To his mother's bower
As dew in April
     That falleth on the
flower.

He came all so still
     There his mother lay,
As dew in April
     That falleth on the spray.

Mother and maiden
     Was never none but she;
Well may such a lady
     Goddes mother be.

ANONYMOUS

PHASE TWO OF THE EXERCISES: *Weeks 6 to 16*

Week 6: The Incarnation and Birth of Jesus

My attitude: God intervened in the history of His people to become one of us and share our lot. In the mystery of my own being and in the story of my own life he is an Advent God, intervening to save me, to love me, to be my companion, and to share my adventure.

What I seek: I ask the Father for three things that I need and only He can give: a more intimate knowledge of Jesus who has become one of us; a more personal experience of His love for me so that I may love Him more tenderly; and a closer union with Jesus in His mission of bringing salvation to His people.

Day 1 of Week 6: The First Contemplation
The Incarnation that gave a human face to divine love.

This contemplation offers two viewpoints: that of the Holy Trinity and that of Mary of Nazareth [101-109]. Here I try to see the world from the perspective of the Three Divine Persons and spend my time in the presence of God my Father, Jesus my brother and their life-giving Spirit. The following excerpt from a document by the 33rd General Congregation of the Society of Jesus provides insights into today's world (nn. 37-38):

> "The *Exercises* invite us to contemplate the world of today with the loving gaze of the Three Divine Persons, that we may be drawn to understand its needs as God does and offer ourselves to share in His work of salvation. . . .Our contemplation of the world reveals a situation frequently hostile to the spreading of the Kingdom. The dominant ideologies and systems—political, economic, social and cultural—often prevent an adequate response to the most elementary aspirations of the human family at both national and international levels. A pervasive materialism and the worship of human autonomy obscure or obliterate concern for the things of God, leaving the minds and hearts of many of our contemporaries cold and empty. This both reveals and causes a profound crisis of faith that expresses itself in an atheism at once theoretical, practical and institutional. Lack of respect for a loving Creator leads to a denial of the dignity of the human person and the wanton destruction of the environment. Massive poverty and hunger, brutal oppression and discrimination, a frightening arms race and the nuclear threat: all offer evidence of sin in human hearts and in the core of contemporary society."

In the first and second exercises of Phase Two [101-109, 110-117], Ignatius describes two very slightly different perspectives with which we may begin this kind of contemplation just described in the Introduction to Phase Two. In the first, we may imagine the perspective of the Father, Son, and Spirit looking upon our world just before the angel Gabriel enters into the scene to announce to Mary the proposed plan for her to become the Mother of God. With God, we watch Mary's response and know that the Son has become man for us. In the second, we may enter into the gospel scene so completely and so personally that we drink in the atmosphere, hear the nuances of what is said, and sense the meaning of gestures and actions at a depth which only a loving presence can penetrate. This is the heart of Ignatian contemplation.

Feel the leap of joy in the heart of God when the decision was made to save this sinful world by the coming to us of the Son.

PREPARATION: It is as always [101], and the GRACE or GIFT THAT I SEEK: for the grace to know Jesus intimately, to love him more intensely, and so to follow him more closely [104].

SETTING: It describes the style of prayer called "contemplation": I try to enter into the vision of God, in his triune life, looking upon our world. . . .The leap of divine joy: God knows that the time has come when the mystery of his salvific plan, hidden from the beginning of the world, will become manifest. The Annunciation scene described by Luke (1: 26-38) portrays Mary's complete, though at first hesitant, but generous response to her Lord and God [102, 103, 106, 107, 108].

COLLOQUY: In it, immersed in this great mystery of God becoming man, I may wish to stay with Mary, or with Jesus, my Savior, who had become a human being for me. Close with an Our Father [109].

Day 2 of Week 6: Luke 1: 26-38
The Annunciation to Mary of God's loving intervention in history.

Both the PREPARATION and the GIFT THAT I SEEK are as in Day 1. The SETTING or the context of the Annunciation scene, is to be found in the text of Scripture. As in the previous meditation I make use of the two approaches to contemplation. (1) I try to see with the eyes of God, and look upon the young girl Mary, as she is greeted by the angel Gabriel. (2) I let myself be totally present to the scene, hearing the nuances of the questions, seeing the expression in the face and eyes, watching the gestures and movements which tell us so much about a person.

The incarnating and then the birthing of Christ represents the beginning of a singular, momentous event in the history of the world and the universe—God becoming a member of the human race. God chose Mary to become the mother of Jesus, and she in turn responded freely to God's invitation. This unique event appeared as commonplace as the birth of any baby in any obscure village in the Middle East. God's subtlety and Mary's understated acquiescence to God's plan, perhaps hardly comprehended, are both models for us to follow with peace and confidence. I notice how our triune God works—so simply and quietly. A world goes on, apparently oblivious of the total revolution which has begun. I look at Mary's complete way of responding to her Lord and God [102,103,106,107,108].

COLLOQUY: As I find myself immersed in the setting of this mystery of the Incarnation, I may want just to stay with Mary or with our Lord, who has now become man for me. Sometimes I may want to speak out my joy, my thanks, my wonder, or my praise. According to the light I have received, I beg for the grace to know and to be able to draw close to Jesus, my Lord. I close the prayer period with an Our Father [109].

Day 3 of Week 6: John 1: 1-18
The Prologue—an overture to the mystery of God become man.

A close reading of the Prologue to John's Gospel and of the Principle and Foundation we experienced in Week 2 of Phase One reveals that the Ignatian statement has a close affinity to the Johanine prologue (Stanley, p. 42). That first chapter of John is an artistically crafted poem in which he first introduces us to the whole Gospel and previews his theology—his beliefs about God and Jesus—and then introduces us to Jesus' ministry. The first eighteen verses summarize the entire twenty-one chapters of John's gospel. As Flanagan notes, the structure in Wisdom 9: 9-12 and Proverbs 8: 22-36 is such that "wisdom personified is first with God, then shares in creation, will come to Earth, and there gift mankind" (CBC, pp. 981-82). John uses this structural pattern of reverse parallelism to repeat these truths in inverse order (1-18):

1. The Word with God (vv. 1-2)   1. The Son at the Father's Side (v. 18)

2. Role in Creation (v.3)   2. Role in re-creation (v.17)

3. Gift to humankind (vv. 4-5)   3. Gift to humankind (v.16)

4. Testimony of John (vv. 6-8)   4. Testimony of John (v.15)

5. The Word enters the World   5. The Incarnation (v. 14)
   (vv. 9-11)

6. Through the Word we become
   children of God (vv. 12-13)

SETTING here is quite abstract and thus does not lend itself as readily to the same kind of prayer as those of previous days. It will be helpful, therefore, to use Ignatius' "Third Method of Prayer" [258-60]. Prayerfully read over the prologue of John's gospel and let God fill me with awe and wonder at the gift of Himself to me and to all His people. This third method of praying consists in my making use of a certain rhythmical flow as I read slowly phrase by phrase or even word by word and reflect on its meaning for me. Making use of the PREPARATION, as always, I reflect upon what I am about to do. The GRACE or GIFT THAT I SEEK is that I may have wisdom so as to appreciate, though I cannot fully understand, the mystery of God having become a human being to save me. The method's attractiveness consists in simply taking the Scriptural passage and relishing its meaning for me.

COLLOQUY: My conversation with God will grow out of my appreciation and gratitude for what this supreme mystery of the Incarnation means to me and to everyone. As always close with a prayer of my own composition, or the Our Father or the Hail Mary.

Day 4 of Week 6: Luke 1: 39–56
Visitation of Our Lady, the Christ bearer, to Elizabeth.

I will use the topical format of previous exercises to contemplate Mary's visit to Elizabeth, trying especially to be alert to the human and divine drama taking place [263]. I will be particularly attentive to Jesus present in the womb of Mary. I will focus attention on and rejoice with Mary as she takes joy in being the Christ-bearer, even though she may not have a very advanced grasp of its implications as yet.

Day 5 of Week 6: Luke 2: 1-20
The Birth of Jesus Christ our Lord.

Attending to the PREPARATION and GIFT THAT I SEEK, I then meditate on the following SETTING [264]: "In the nativity of Jesus at Bethlehem, the mystery presented by Ignatius as the second exercise in this series, he expands the simple scripture setting by relating the circumstances of Jesus' birth to a comprehensive view of his life of hardship leading to death on a cross. The simple way that Ignatius would call each retreatant to be fully present within a particular mystery of Christ's life is at the same time made more whole or integrated by his suggestions for expanding realistically the perspectives as, for example, from the viewpoint of God or from the viewpoint of Christ's whole life leading up to his death on the cross for us." (Fleming, 1973, p.10).

The events related by Luke in the second chapter are private, hidden and local, but they will be significant for the whole world, especially for the poor, the outcasts, and the disenfranchised who were ready for Christ's "Good News." Luke notes the swaddling clothes and the manger—for their special meaning. The manger, a feeding trough for animals, subtly reminds us of the poverty and humility of Jesus' birth, but the wrappings are a veiled reference to his royalty. Here is a parallel to the birth of Solomon, King David's son, "In swaddling clothes and with constant care I was nurtured. For no king has any different origin or birth" (Wis 7: 45).

The second part of the narrative, the announcement of Jesus' birth to the shepherds is in harmony with Luke's theme that the lowly who are of good will are to be singled out as the recipients of God's favors and blessings (see also Lk 1:48, 52 & NAB, pp. 122–23). Luke regards Jesus as savior—as the one who rescues all humans from sin and frees humanity from the condition of alienation from God.

COLLOQUY: Peacefully present at His birth, I receive Jesus with joy and gratitude as the Father's gift to me and to His people, simply gazing upon God-become-man.

Day 6 of Week 6: Matthew 1: 18–25
"Now this is how the birth of Jesus Christ came about."

In this contemplation I return to the birth of Jesus, but following Ignatius' directions [110], I let my fantasy dwell upon all the details of His coming among us so that the event may become all the more meaningful for me. This means that my PREPARATION for [110], as well as the GRACE [113] from contemplation will be as always.

SETTING: It is described for me by the Evangelist. But with the eye of the imagination I see the details of the situation, such as the road over which Mary and Joseph travelled, the place to which Joseph took Mary when there was no room for them at the inn, where she was to give birth to the Savior of the World [111, 112, 114, 115, 116].

I should take note of the hardship which is already so much a part of Jesus' presence in our world. The labors of the journey to Bethlehem, the struggles of finding a shelter, the poverty, hunger, thirst, heat and cold, the insults which meet the arrival of God-with-us—all this that he might die on the cross for me.

COLLOQUY or Spontaneous Prayer: According to the different aspects upon which I may focus at any one time within the prayer period, for example, I respond variously to Mary, to Joseph, to Jesus, to the Father and to the Holy Spirit. There may be little to "say" because this style of contemplation is often more a "being with" experience than a word-response [117].

—— *61* ——

As always I bring the period of prayer to a close with a Hail Mary or some other prayer appropriate to the subject matter.

Day 7 of Week 6: Repetition
A "letting go" or total immersion of myself.

Ignatius makes much of the importance of the repetition of ideas or points that have evoked a special response from me during the preceding contemplations. As often as I find that I would like to return to a particular mystery it is always important to return to those parts or focal points where I have experienced understanding, consolation, or desolation [118].

Since the entrance into the setting of such a repetition is frequently very simple, the emphasis more and more is fixed on my personal response which is represented by spontaneous prayer. I should always remember to close the prayer period reverently with an Our Father.

In this REPETITION and in all those which follow, the usual way of proceeding is observed as was explained in the First Week. The subject matter changes, but the same manner of repeating the exercise continues [119].

In addition to the Repetition Ignatius recommends a kind of repetition that he refers to as an APPLICATION OF THE SENSES. After the preparatory prayer and the petition for the usual grace, this last period of prayer within the Week is meant to be a "letting go," a total immersion of myself into the mystery of Christ's life this day, so that I may thereby become not only more Christlike but more my true self. The notion here is to build upon all the experiences which have been a part of my day or week of prayer. Again, it is akin to the passive way my senses take in sights, smells, sounds, feelings, as an automatic datum for my attention. The total felt-environment of the particular mystery of Christ's life, in whatever ways it can be most vividly mine, is the setting for this final period of prayer in each week [122, 123, 124, 125].

COLLOQUY: I respond as I am so moved by God's grace. I close with an Our Father.

A Child my Choice

Let folly praise that fancy loves, I praise and love that child,
Whose heart no thought, whose tongue no word, whose hand no deed
defiled.
I praise him most, I love him best, all praise and love is his;
While him I love, in him I live, and cannot live amiss.

Love's sweetest mark, laud's highest theme, man's most desired light,
To love him life, to leave him death, to live in him delight.
He mine by gift, I his by debt, thus each to other due.
First friend he was, best friend he is, all times will try him true.

Though young, yet wise, though small, yet strong; though man, yet
God he is;
As wise he knows, as strong he can, as God he loves to bless.
His knowledge rules, his strength defends, his love doth cherish all;
His birth our joy, his life our light, his death our end of thrall.

Alas! He weeps, he sighs, he pants, yet do his angels sing;
Out of his tears, his sighs and throbs, doth bud a joyful spring.
Almighty Babe, whose tender arms can force all foes to fly,
Correct my faults, protect my life, direct me when I die.

ROBERT SOUTHWELL, S.J.

Week 7: The "Showing Forth" of the Newborn King

My perception of my Companion and King

My perception is that of the author of Hebrews who in the prologue to his letter says (1: 1-3):

> **1.** In times past, God spoke in partial and various ways to our ancestors through the prophets;
> **2.** in these last days, he spoke to us through a son, whom he made heir of all things and through whom he created the universe,
> **3.** who is the refulgence of his glory, the very imprint of his being, and who sustains all things by his mighty word. When he had accomplished purification from sins, he took his seat at the right hand of the Majesty on high,. . .

By this stage you, the retreatant, may be expected to have developed a fairly systematic approach to prayer that will include the PREPARATION, that is always basically the same, the GIFT that you seek that is closely related to a closer union with Jesus, and finally the resulting COLLOQUY. The SETTING is that part of the prayer that may change with each day.

The gift I seek: I beg the Father so to draw me to His son Jesus, now manifested to the nations, that my awareness of Him may become deeper, my experience of His love more intense, and my desire to follow Him more passionate.

Day 1 of Week 7: Luke 2: 8-18
"I proclaim to you good news of great joy that will be for all the people."

The humble King's birth is announced first to the shepherds, who generally were considered as poor, verging on being outcasts, and regarded by their "betters" as ignorant, dirty and lawless. It is a depressing fact worldwide that in almost every walk of life there are insiders and outsiders—those who are "in" can thrive in the system and those who are "out" can buck the tide or are overwhelmed by the system. In Old Testament times, Yahweh, the God of Israel, looked after his chosen people as a Father. However, in God's providence, Jesus came on Earth to fulfil and enlarge access to the divine life, to salvation on the part of everyone. Jesus made it abundantly clear in his teaching that the poor, the downtrodden, the sick and the disadvantaged were the insiders in his Kingdom, but that none were outsiders except by their own choice. The paradox is the wisdom by which the people of God live: "Blessed are the poor in spirit, the reign of God is theirs."

I yearn to encounter Jesus with the simplicity and the directness of the shepherds. COLLOQUY: Let it express this yearning.

Day 2 of Week 7: Luke 2: 19–38
Jesus is presented to the Lord in the Temple.

The parents of Jesus obeyed the Roman law at the time of his birth. Now they are seen to be observant Jews fulfilling the prescriptions of the religious law relating to circumcision and the presentation of the first-born to the Lord. Luke's emphasis is more on the presentation of Jesus in the temple than on the purification of Mary. His emphasis on their poverty prompts him to mention that Mary and Joseph offer a pair of turtledoves or two young pigeons.

Mary, unable to fully understand the significance of the good news announced by the angel and of God's action that involved her son, Jesus, rolls these events around in her mind. The verse (Lk 2: 19), "And Mary kept all these things, reflecting on them in her heart" recurs as a refrain yet again "and his mother kept all these things in her heart" (Lk 2: 51). These phrases tell us a good deal about Mary, the model believer and her progress in faith, as do other passages in Luke such as 8: 19-21 and 11: 27-29 as well as those in Acts 1: 14. Each one of us has embarked on a journey of faith and we may ask of Mary, "how can this be accomplished since I do not know where it is leading and I am fearful of the consequences?" Look to Mary, the model believer, and ask her to help you in your unbelief.

Day 3 of Week 7: Mankind's evolving "noosphere"
How we as individuals can participate significantly in hastening the coming of Christ's Kingdom.

In the Epilogue to *The Divine Milieu*, Teilhard de Chardin summarizes his view of how we as individuals can participate significantly in hastening the coming of Christ's Kingdom. He uses the following concepts that I believe will be helpful.

Teilhard, as a geologist, recognized the several spheres that form the outer shell of the earth, one of which is most significant to the topic at hand. The lithosphere, made of rock, supports the hydrosphere, made of water—the ocean, the lakes, and other waterways. Those two in turn are intimately associated with the biosphere and the atmosphere. But Teilhard as a Christian also recognized another, a spiritual sphere. Forming since the time of mankind's appearance on Earth, it consists of the products of mind and heart. Teilhard called it "noosphere," from the Greek word, *nous*, meaning mind.

He believed, and I believe, that each of us contributes to the formation of this sphere every time we use mind or heart. In part, this noosphere consists of tangible things—books, computers, schools, shovels and axes. In part, it consists of intangibles--our thoughts, our love, our good wishes, and even our disappointments, pain, and suffering. As workers in this world who intend to do so, we build up the noosphere, which is related to the Kingdom of God. What we do on Sunday and what we do the rest of the week are all basically part of the same sacred activity.

Teilhard's view is that each companion of Jesus participates both in dissipating the evil elements of the world and in refining and purifying the beneficial elements through work and suffering. That twofold participation is, in effect, described in Malachi 3: 2-3. Teilhard amplifies on how we can contribute to the evolving noosphere:

> Under the influence of this twofold movement, which is still almost entirely hidden, the universe is being transformed and is maturing all around us. . . .One day, the Gospel tells us, the tension gradually accumulating between humanity and God will touch the limits prescribed by the possibilities of the world. . . .Then the presence of Christ, which has been silently accruing in things, will suddenly be revealed—like a flash of light from pole to pole. . .it will invade the face of the earth. . .and will occupy. . .under the influence of Christ, the place of happiness or pain designated for them by the living structure of the Pleroma (meaning complete fulfilment). . . .Such will be the consummation of the divine *milieu*.

A key element in Teilhard's view is that we must expect the coming of the Kingdom and ardently desire it:

> The Israelites were constantly expectant, and the first Christians too. Christmas, which might have been thought to turn our gaze towards the past, has only fixed it further in the future. The Messiah, who appeared for a moment in our midst, only allowed himself to be seen and touched for a moment before vanishing once again, more luminous and ineffable than ever. . . .The Lord Jesus will only come soon if we ardently expect him. It is an accumulation of desires that should cause the Pleroma to burst upon us.

A fearless optimism should be ours based on the attraction of Christ on us, His members, and our perception that there is an intimate connection between the victory of Christ and the outcome of our work.

Day 4 of Week 7: Decree on the Apostolate of the Laity (DAL)
Our Co-responsibility for Christ's Mission.

The renewal of the Church called for in the documents of the Council depends in great part on a laity who fully understand not only the documents of Vatican II but also their own co-responsibility for the mission of Christ in the Church and in the world. It is clear that the call to great adventure with Christ our King has been given to the laity as well as to the clergy. The Decree on the Apostolate of the Laity goes on to say (Nos. 1-3):

> The layman's apostolate derives from his Christian vocation, and the Church can never be without it. Sacred Scripture clearly shows how spontaneous and fruitful such activity was at the very beginning of the Church (cf. Acts 11:19-21; 18:26; Rom 16:1-16; Phil 4:3). . . . Our own times require of the laity no less zeal. In fact, modern conditions demand that their apostolate be thoroughly broadened and intensified. . . . An indication of this manifold and pressing need is the unmistakable work of the Holy Spirit in making the laity today even more conscious of their own responsibility and inspiring them everywhere to serve Christ and the Church. . . .
>
> For this the Church was founded: that by spreading the kingdom of Christ everywhere for the glory of God the Father, she might bring all to share in Christ's saving redemption; and that through them the whole world might in actual fact be brought into relationship with Him. All activity of the Mystical Body directed to the attainment of this goal is called the apostolate, and the Church carries it on in various ways through all her members. For by its very nature the Christian vocation is also a vocation to the apostolate. . . . They exercise a genuine apostolate by their activity on behalf of bringing the gospel and holiness to mankind, and on behalf of penetrating and perfecting the temporal sphere of things through the spirit of the gospel. In this way their temporal activity can openly bear witness to Christ and promote the salvation of mankind. . . .
>
> Incorporated into Christ's Mystical Body through baptism and strengthened by the power of the Holy Spirit through confirmation, they are assigned to the apostolate by the Lord himself. They are consecrated into a royal priesthood and a holy people (cf. 1 Pet. 2:4-10) in order that they may offer spiritual sacrifices through everything they do, and may witness to Christ throughout the world. For their part, the sacraments, especially the most holy Eucharist, communicate and nourish that charity which is the soul of the entire apostolate (DAL, pp. 489-92).

Younger people should feel that this call has been directed to them in particular, and they should respond to it eagerly and magnanimously.

COLLOQUY: In a fourfold conversation express your gratitude for having been called to the apostolate by baptism, and for the fact that this invitation has been made explicit in the conciliar decree. Speak to Mary, the Mother of Jesus and of his mystical body, the people of God. Converse with Jesus on behalf of whose mystical body you are called to "share in the priestly, prophetic and royal office." Bring your concerns and gratitude to your Father, in whose master plan you participate and who draws you to himself. And finally, pray to the Holy Spirit who diffuses in the hearts of all members of the Church the faith, hope and charity through which the apostolate is carried on (Jn 17: 3; 1 Cor 12: 7).

Day 5 of Week 7: Matthew 2: 1–12
"We saw his star at its rising and have come to do him homage."

FOCUS: the great faith called forth in the Magi. In this section of Chapter 2 Matthew records one of four episodes that deal with places—the focus here being on Bethlehem. Both the prophet and the author of the second book of Samuel had referred to the birthplace of the Messiah (Mi 5: 1; 2 Sm 5: 2). "And you, Bethlehem, land of Judah, are by no means least among the rulers of Judah; since from you shall come a ruler, who is to shepherd my people Israel (Mt 2: 6)." So this reference to the Old Testament passages suggests that the Messiah's itinerary recounted in Matthew's chapter was guided by the will of God (CBC, Harrington, p. 865).

Day 6 of Week 7: Luke 2: 22–38
The Purification of Our Lady and the Presentation of the Child Jesus.

FOCUS: the examples of Mary, Jesus, Simeon, and Anna are each a call to faith. Any new mother of a son who could not afford a lamb for her purification could offer two turtledoves instead, as Mary does here on the occasion of the consecration of her firstborn son (Lk 2: 22-24), a requirement of the law (Ex 13: 2, 12). We are reminded of the devout presentation in the temple of the boy Samuel where Hannah offers him for sanctuary service (1 Sm 1: 24-28). Luke explains how the birth of Jesus brings Simeon's and Anna's hopes and expectations for redemption of Jerusalem to fulfilment (Lk 2: 25-38).

The gratitude of Simeon for God's graciousness in letting his eyes see God's "salvation which you prepared in sight of all the peoples, a light for revelation to the Gentiles, and glory for your people Israel" (Lk 2: 31-32), is a model of faith, hope, and love for each of us. But more than that, our gratitude should be very great because we are included among those for whom salvation has been prepared.

Although it was not required that Jesus be presented in the Temple in Jerusalem, it is interesting that he returned there when he was twelve years old, and again in the final days before his passion, death, and resurrection. Simeon made the cryptic prediction, "Behold, this child is destined for the fall and rise of many in Israel, and to be a sign that will be contradicted (and you yourself a sword will pierce) so that the thoughts of many hearts may be revealed" (Lk 2: 34-35). This prediction may take on a personal meaning in light of the insight that the shadow of the cross falls across the path of all those who present themselves in the service of Jesus.

COLLOQUY: It expresses heartfelt gratitude and is here adapted from the classic colloquy of Simeon (in turn adapted from the great Book of Isaiah (Is 52: 9-10; 49: 6; 46: 13; 42: 6; 40: 5). It may well reflect your own expression of gratitude.

Day 7 of Week 7: Repetition
Place yourself once more in the nativity events.

Return to those aspects of the meditations of the week that have proved most fruitful. It may be helpful to approach some of the scenes, such as the Birth of Jesus, using the application of the senses, previously recommended in earlier exercises. Place yourself in the scene and, if possible, picture vividly the persons, their actions, words, and attitudes so that you may learn about their sincerity. Pray to some of the principals, asking them to strengthen your growth in sincerity, in prayerfulness, and in an attitude of homage to the infant Son of God, your brother.

O Shut Your Bright Eyes

O shut your bright eyes that mine must endanger
With their watchfulness; protected by its shade
Escape from my care: what can you discover
From my tender look but how to be afraid?
Love can but confirm the more it would deny.
 Close your bright eye.

Sleep. What have you learned from the womb that bore you
But an anxiety your Father cannot feel?
Sleep. What will the flesh that I gave do for you,
Or my mother love, but tempt you from His will?
Why was I chosen to teach His Son to weep?
 Little One, sleep.

Dream. In human dreams earth ascends to Heaven
Where no one need pray nor ever feel alone.
In your first few hours of life here, O have you
Chosen already what death must be your own?
How soon will you start on the Sorrowful Way?
 Dream while you may.

W. H. AUDEN

Week 8: *The Hidden Life of Jesus*

Considerations for a Contemplative in Action Today

My attitude: Let my attitude be that of seeking a loving, maturing relationship with Mary and Joseph and with the Father, as we may presume Jesus did in his hidden life in Nazareth. May my attitude be that of the psalmist who sings in Praise of God's Law: "How shall a young man be faultless in his way? By keeping to your words. With all my heart I seek you; let me not stray from your commands. Within my heart I treasure your promise, that I may not sin against you (Psalm 119, vv.9-11)."

What I seek: I beg the Father to draw me to His son Jesus so that with eyes fixed on Him, I may come to know Him more intimately, to experience His love more profoundly, and be more closely one with Him in serving God's people.

Day 1 of Week 8: Matthew 2: 13–18
Joseph's flight into Egypt with Mary and Jesus.

The story of the flight into Egypt [269] is similar to that of the story of Jesus' birth in that it consists of an angel's appearance to Joseph in a dream, a command, a reason for the command, Joseph's determination to carry out the command, and a quotation from the Old Testament (Hos 11: 1). Egypt was a place of refuge for Jews at that time, and only upon the death of Herod in 4 B.C. was it safe for Joseph to bring Jesus and Mary back to Nazareth. The quotation from Hosea, "Out of Egypt I called my son" indicates that this episode in the life of Jesus was understood to represent God's will (Mt 2: 15). Moreover, it not only identifies Jesus as the Son of God but suggests that he personifies the people of God. Just as God called Israel out of Egypt in the Exodus so as to create a special people for himself, so he calls Jesus out of Egypt into the land of Israel in order to create a new people. "Out of Egypt" refers to the basic experience of salvation, the exodus from Egyptian bondage. Thus the principle of continuity between the old and new people of God is Jesus the Jew, (CBC, Harrington, pp. 865-66). We see reflected here central features of Matthew's theology, namely the title of Jesus Son of God and Son of David. As such, Jesus is seen as the new Solomon, with connotations of healer and wise man (NJBC, Viviano, p. 631).

I contemplate Jesus, a refugee from his homeland, totally dependent on Joseph and Mary for his human survival, confident that his Father's providential care guides his life. And they depended so totally on God that even in dreams they discerned his voice.

Day 2 of Week 8: Matthew 2: 19-23
"Take the child and his mother and go to the land of Israel."

This narrative passage [270] and that of Day 1 of this week have a special significance in our own times because of the widespread proliferation of refugees and other displaced persons in many parts of the world. Unfortunately the Herods of this world are alive, well, and without compassion or wisdom.

Let us picture ourselves as a part of this Holy Family experiencing the hardship of displacement and taking up a new life in a place other than that which was their first choice. Experience the frustrations of each member of that family. Can I relate to this in terms of my own experience to some degree? How do they deal with these frustrations? Can I learn from each one, Jesus, Mary and Joseph? I will speak to them and ask for guidance as I seek wisdom so that I may be of help in bringing some degree of acceptance to refugees and displaced persons. I pray that some of the wisdom of Solomon and the strength of Samson be given to me so that I may better be able to bring Jesus to my part of the Kingdom.

Day 3 of Week 8: Luke 2: 41-49
Jesus goes up to the temple at age twelve.

Luke's love and esteem for that holy place impelled him to begin his narrative in the temple (1: 5-25) and conclude the overture there [272]. The temple is also where the third gospel ends—with the disciples "continually in the temple praising God" (Lk 24: 53). This entire story leads us to the first recorded words of Jesus. Previously Jesus' identity had been characterized by Gabriel, Mary, Zechariah, Simeon, or angels, but in these words of his own, Jesus tells us who he is. The "must" theme, referring to those elements of Jesus' life which represent his Father's will for him, emerges here, "Did you not know that I must be in my Father's house?" which may also be translated "Did you not know that I must be about my Father's work?" Jesus finds the Temple a comfortable place. It is, after all, his Father's house. I want to be with Him in His youthful zest for the things of God, and I invite Him to be with me as I go about my Father's business. Jesus refers to God as his Father, to his divine sonship, and to his obedience to his heavenly Father's will as taking precedence over his family ties to Joseph and Mary.

Every mother, who takes the time to look upon her child and speculate what life may have in store, can relate to the Scriptural passage that tells of Mary's reflections on what all of these events may mean. As a mother she would wish to protect her son from fear, from anxiety, from death, and from all the distress that lies between birth and death. But she also knows that she plays an important, but limited part in helping to nourish the child who is to grow to adulthood, prepared for the rest of life's work.

Day 4 of Week 8: Matthew 2: 23, Luke 2: 39–40, 2: 50–52
The life of Christ Our Lord from the age of twelve to the age of thirty.

Today, as I contemplate Jesus living and working in Nazareth [272], I may wonder about such things as: When did Mary first tell Him the story of his birth and of the crowded inns and empty stables? How did she teach Him about God the Father? How did the thought of His future mission take shape? Why did He spend most of the years of his life in obscurity?

Mary and Joseph did not understand that Jesus believed that the work of his Father should take precedence over his family relationship to them in Nazareth. Perhaps Simeon's words "and you yourself a sword will pierce" may have come back to have special meaning after Jesus was found in the temple after three days of searching for the son who was lost.

These scenes have obvious implications for our own lives, and especially in situations to which the eyes of faith alone can discern the appropriate response. Let us respond prayerfully to the people and situations involved and reverently enter into colloquy with those to whom we are moved to speak and ask for help in developing our own spirituality.

Day 5 of Week 8: The Divinization of our Activities
Emulating Christ in our own "hidden life."

Among other considerations reflect on what motivated Jesus to live and work so long as a carpenter before entering his "career." How did he spend his days, his years? A good deal of every person's life, no matter how active, is carried out in private, or at least few really know about it or care about it in detail. Thus, in large part, each of us lives the "hidden life" analogously to that of Jesus from age 12 to 30. During that time he must have learned to pray, a most important feature of his later life as well, and to develop so many other facets of his life that are important for us to emulate. Pray meditatively over the following phrases or concepts modified from *The Divine Milieu* (pp. 62-70):

We may, perhaps, imagine that creation was finished long ago. But that would be quite wrong. It continues still more magnificently, and at the highest levels of the world. . . .And we serve to complete it, even by the humblest work of our hands. . . .Owing to the interrelation between matter, soul and Christ, we bring part of the being which he desires back to God *in whatever we do*. With each one of our works. . .we bring to Christ a little fulfillment. . . .

In action. . .I adhere to the creative power of God; I become not only the instrument but its living extension. . .I merge myself, in a sense, through my heart, with the very heart of God. . . .The will to succeed, a certain passionate delight in the work to be done, form an integral part of our creaturely fidelity. . . . Any increase (in the relationship between natural and supernatural actions in the world) is translated into some increase in my power to love and some progress in Christ's blessed hold upon the Universe.

Also read in *The Divine Milieu* the relevant sections in Part One: "Communion through Action" (No. 4), and "the Christian Perfection of Human Endeavor" (No. 5).

Day 6 of Week 8: Luke 2: 52
"Jesus advanced [in] wisdom and age and favor before God and Man."

In the meditation for Day 1 of Week 8 we saw that Jesus is presented, along with other important titles, as the new Solomon, because of his wisdom. Solomon, who "loved the Lord," endeared himself to God and to generations of Scripture readers ever since because he petitioned God in a dream for an understanding heart, in response to the Lord's spontaneous statement at Gibeon, "Ask something of me and I will give it to you" (1 Kgs 3: 5). "I do as you requested. I give you a heart so wise and understanding that there has never been anyone like you up to now, and after you there will come no one to equal you," said the Lord (1 Kgs 3: 12).

Jesus, during his "hidden" years in Nazareth, must often have meditated upon the books of Wisdom, of Proverbs, and Sirach, gaining inspiration and strength from them. Let us prize and cherish wisdom above all other possessions, and pray earnestly, for an understanding heart, for wisdom, as did Solomon.

Day 7 of Week 8: Application of the Senses
Use the Scriptural passages cited this week—namely those on the life of Christ between ages twelve to thirty.

The following piece was written by one of my former retreatants and has been a favorite with many subsequent participants because it captures the spirit of the hidden life of a contemplative in action in a modern setting:

My Hidden Life in the Cathedral of My Home

How far must one travel to pray in some of the beautiful cathedrals? How many of us are confined temporarily or permanently to our own little corner of this world and cannot travel? Well, look around, look around, and dream and pray.

Recently a long illness prevented me from going to church. Feeling poorly and incapable of being about my usual busy-ness, depression took over—and then self pity, worse than the disease itself, crept in! I was alone in a house that was usually filled with love and living. The quiet was overpowering. Tearfully, I stood in my kitchen when out of the depths came spiritual help.

I thought: "This is not an empty house. This can be my very own cathedral. Lord, come into my home and bring your Mother and all the angels and saints who are not too busy with other people's problems."

My cathedral is well equipped. Here in my kitchen there are three altars: the sink, the stove, and the ironing board. How many sacrifices can be offered standing there talking to my heavenly guests! Walking to the bedroom, I find a Chapel where, even on busy days, the quiet solitude lends itself to prayer and meditation and rest. The bathroom is the baptismal room where flowing waters cleanse the body as well as the soul.

At 9:30 a.m. a flick of the switch. . .there is the TV Mass in my living room. In this, the main part of my Cathedral, there are no stained glass windows, just stained windows from lack of recent housework, but the sunshine found its way in, hit a prism on a lamp and danced in pretty colors on the rug. From outside I could hear a heavenly choir. The birds were in full voice!

At noon time, chimes rang out from the clock on the steeple of my mantlepiece and announced it was time for the Angelus. I was not alone for lunch; didn't take count of how many spiritual guests were there; maybe twelve, even thirteen, but I lit the candles and we broke bread together.

Suddenly the silence was broken and in bounced a granddaughter for an unexpected visit. "Do you got some ice cream, Nana?" My Cathedral even has a social hall.

MARION G. HORNE

You, neighbor God

You, neighbour God, if sometimes in the night
I rouse you with loud knocking, I do so
only because I seldom hear you breathe;
I know; you are alone.
And should you need a drink, no one is there
to reach it to you, groping in the dark.
Always I hearken. Give but a small sign.
I am quite near.

Between us there is but a narrow wall,
and by sheer chance; for it would take
merely a call from your lips or from mine
to break it down,
and that without a sound.

The wall is builded of your images.

They stand before you hiding you like names,
And when the light within me blazes high
that in my inmost soul I know you by,
the radiance is squandered on their flames.

And then my senses, which too soon grow lame,
exiled from you, must go their homeless ways.

RAINER MARIA RILKE

Week 9: *The Strategy of Jesus*

In summing up the strategy of Jesus in a phrase, we are confronted by the need to think globally on the one hand, and locally and right down to our nearest neighbor on the other hand. "I have come to cast fire on the earth; and what will I but that it be enkindled!" "As long as you did it for one of the least of my brothers (or sisters, as Jesus would say nowadays), you did it for me." But the blueprint of his strategy is not that clearly discerned; the enemy has obstructed our vision and sometimes we grope in the dark trying to get enough light to read our roadmap. But we have the wisdom of the guiding Spirit as the light to discern his strategy and distinguish it from the Deceiver's.

Experiences of Consolation and Desolation

My attitude: That of Ignatius as he spoke of himself in his journal:

> It often happened that on a bright day [Ignatius] could see something in the air near him; because it was indeed very beautiful, it gave him great comfort. He could not discern very well the kind of thing it was, but in a way it seemed to him to have the form of a serpent with many things which shone like eyes, though they were not eyes. He found great pleasure and consolation in seeing this thing, and the more he saw it the more his consolation increased. When it disappeared he was saddened.
>
> Until this time he had remained always in nearly the same interior state of great and steady happiness without having any knowledge of the inward things of the spirit. During those days while the vision lasted or somewhat before it began (for it lasted many days), a harsh thought came to trouble him by pointing out the hardship of his life, as if someone was saying within his soul, "How will you be able to endure this life for the seventy years you yet have to live?" Believing that the thought came from the enemy, he answered inwardly with great vehemence, "Oh miserable being! Can you promise me an hour of life?" So he overcame the temptation and remained at peace. . . .
>
> But soon after the temptations noted above he began to experience great changes in his soul. Sometimes he found himself so disagreeable that he took no joy in prayer or hearing mass or in any other prayer he said. At other times exactly the opposite of this came over him so suddenly that he seemed to have thrown off sadness and desolation just as one snatches a cape from another's shoulders. Here he began to be astounded by these changes he had never experienced before. . . .From the lessons God had given him he now had some experience of the diversity of spirits and he began to wonder about the means by which the spirit had come. . . .God treated him at this time just as a schoolmaster treats a child whom he is teaching.

He went to kneel before a nearby cross to give thanks to God. There, the vision that had appeared to him many times but which he had never understood, that is, the thing mentioned above which seemed very beautiful to him and had many eyes, now appeared to him. But while kneeling before the cross, he saw clearly that the object did not have its usual beautiful color, and with a strong affirmation of his will he knew very clearly that it came from the demon. For a long time it often appeared to him, but as a sign of contempt he drove it away with a staff he used to carry in his hand (O'Callaghan, pp. 33-40).

The Grace or the gift I seek: As a brother or sister of Ignatius I ask God to let me share in the gift given to Ignatius of being able to recognize the deceits of Satan and to guard myself against them; and I also ask for a true knowledge of Jesus Christ, my true Leader and Lord, and the grace to imitate Him.

Day 1 of Week 9: Meditation
On the Two Leaders and two totally different strategies.

As we consider Christ, our Leader and Lord, our God and Brother, and we consider Satan, the personal enemy who sums up all the evils that beset mankind [136], we make the usual PREPARATION. The GRACE [139], the SETTING [137, 138, 140-46], and the quadruple COLLOQUY have been elaborated and summarized previously and again, in part, below.

SETTING: The first part, which consists of shedding light upon the forces of evil in the person of Satan, makes me face the enormous power and oppression of evil itself. I try to grasp the strategy of Satan as he attempts ever to enslave men and women and the world according to his design. From such honor arises the false sense of identity and value in which false pride has its roots. The more important second part of the Setting consists of looking at Jesus Christ who calls himself "the way, the truth and the life," and noticing how gently but insistently, Jesus continues to call followers of all kinds and to send them forth to spread his good news to all people, no matter what their state or condition. Jesus' strategy is to try to help people, not enslave or oppress them. The result will be a life of true humility [143, 144, 145, 146], with Jesus Christ my only possession.

COLLOQUY: I enter into the intensity of the prayer by addressing Mary, Christ, the Holy Spirit, and the Father begging from them the insights and strength that I need.

Days 2 and 3 of Week 9: Repetition
Again, the Two Leaders and their strategies.

Because this exercise focuses on the importance of discernment in discriminating between the "finger of God" and the "tail of the Serpent," it is made several times during this week, with the same colloquies [148]. I will especially consider three temptations in the strategy of the adversary: greed, anger, and delusion. I shall also ponder the three steps in the strategy of Jesus: poverty, insults, and humility. These steps imply a surrender of control over aspects of life that most people let go of reluctantly.

Ignatian discernment is central to the work of discovering the will of God and even of "finding God in all things." It is, moreover, also firmly rooted in the Evangelist John's insights into the role of the Holy Spirit. Stanley carefully elaborates several Paraclete-sayings that help greatly in relating the role of the Holy Spirit to Ignatian discernment (pp. 234–39). The first of these sayings concerns the assurances in Mark "that it will not be you who are speaking but the holy Spirit" (13: 9-11) and in "When the Paraclete, Whom I shall send to you from the Father, comes, He will bear witness concerning me; but you yourselves also bear witness, because you have been in my company from the beginning" (16: 26-27).

This saying is part of the "remembering" that the apostolic community carried on with the help of the Paraclete: "The Advocate, the holy spirit that the Father will send in my name—he will teach you everything and remind you of all that I told you." Once launched on the work of the risen Lord, the disciples discover that their word is efficacious, as Jesus prayed that it would be (Jn 17: 20), because their personal experience from the beginning of Jesus' public ministry will be supported by the Paraclete. "It was this intuition into the real nature of an apostolic vocation by Ignatius that convinced him that there cannot be any real dichotomy between an active and a contemplative vocation" (Stanley, pp. 234–35).

In the Gospels we read that the disciples were followers of Jesus since he was there in person to assist them with decisions as to how to conduct their lives. St. Ignatius looks on spiritual discernment as an analog because we have the assurance that Jesus has sent the Paraclete to guide future generations who are attentive to two areas prominent in Ignatian discernment: (1) guidance in progressively seeking the will of God, and (2) attention to the earthly life of Jesus as the unique source of the definitive revelation of the invisible Father. "I have much more to tell you, but you cannot bear it now. But when he comes, the Spirit of truth, he will guide you to all truth". . . .(Jn 16: 12-15). As did Paul: "Each person will bear his own load" (Gal 6: 5), Ignatius calls on us: to fulfill the law of Christ in the Principle and Foundation (Week 2, [23]); in the Call of the King (Week 5, [98]); and in the strategy of the Two Leaders (Week 9, [147-48]).

The role of the Paraclete in the discernment process is further clarified, "He will guide you along the way by the entire truth." Jesus remains "the way," the unique way to the Father "through" him (Jn 14: 6). "The Paraclete's role is not to bring any new or additional revelation. . . .He will reveal to the community in every age how Jesus' message is to be lived out faithfully no matter what may occur. . .This ultimately means the disclosure of the unseen God—'All the Father has is mine'—the ultimate reason why 'the Word became flesh'. . .This crucially important Ignatian teaching on discernment is exemplified in the great care taken by Ignatius to remind the exercitant, to measure such spiritual experiences against certain objective norms. The earthly life of Jesus, as reported in the Gospels, . . .contains that 'true teaching of Christ our Lord,' with which the retreatant must be 'inflamed' before entering upon the elections [164]. For this reason too he counsels that the practice of discernment be carried out 'at the same time as we contemplate his (Jesus') life' [135]" (Stanley, p. 237).

Day 4 of Week 9: Repetition
The Touch of God and the Tail of the Serpent.

This exercise is a repetition of the Meditation on the Two Leaders and their Strategies with additional suggestions that have as their goal to develop in each of us a great sensitivity to the deceits of Satan (the Evil Spirit) and to the authentic movements of the Holy Spirit. Greed, in all its forms, anger, hatred, and delusion are so readily perceived as good and their opposite as unenlightened or "wimpy" that we need guidelines and a model by which to sort out these elements in our life. To do this we need to develop a deep silence and peace in the depths of ourselves so that we can discriminate between the touch of God and that of Satan. Following Jesus and the Buddha, both of whom in their discourses speak of the Spirit of evil in the world as a person, Ignatius calls on us to recognize that all mankind follows one leader or the other and that we are called to dedicated service in the following of our leader, Jesus Christ.

Day 5 of Week 9: Meditation
Three Types of Persons.

This is a meditation to aid me in my freedom of choice according to God's call to me [149]. The PREPARATION is as always, and the GRACE or GIFT that I seek is that I may be free enough to choose whatever the lead of God's grace may indicate as his particular call to me [152]. The SETTING [150, 151] is devoted to a consideration of three types of persons. Each one of them has taken in quite a few possessions—not always with the best of motives, and in fact sometimes quite selfishly. In general, each one is a good person, and he would like to serve God, even to the extent that if these possessions were to come in the way of his salvation, he would like to be free of them [150, 151]. Of these three types, the first is "a lot of talk, but no action" [153]; the second is willing "to do everything but the one thing necessary" [154]; the third reflects a complete generosity toward God, "to do Your will is my desire" [155].

COLLOQUY: This is the same quadruple colloquy or conversation as in the previous days [159M].

We may find it helpful at this time of the retreat when we might discover some attachment opposed to actual poverty or a repugnance to it, or when we are not indifferent to poverty and riches, to come to Jesus our Lord in prayer and beg him to choose us to serve him in actual poverty. We should beg with a certain insistence, and we should plead for it—but always wanting what God wants for us [157].

Day 6 of Week 9: Luke 4: 1-13; Matthew 4: 1-11
The Temptation of Christ.

FOCUS: the reality of temptation is present in the calling of Christ [161] and in turn in his calls to the apostles—and to us [274].

The tactics of the adversary are to tempt Jesus not to evil but to be a Messiah of possessions, prestige, and power, instead of the Messiah of poverty, persecution, and powerlessness that the Father called Him to be. Luke places the final temptation of this series in Jerusalem. When Jesus is on the cross in Jerusalem (Lk 23: 34-39), he will again experience temptations similar to those earlier ones (Lk 4: 1-13); and He will overcome them and all evil by his faith.

In modern society it is commonplace to dismiss the reality of temptation and all the more so, sin itself, as chimerical. The fact that Jesus, the incarnate God, was subjected to temptations throughout his life and especially in his passion and death, should be of great consolation to us who are also subject to them. However, we must take courage and strength from the assurance that Jesus has chosen us and not we who have chosen him. We have the sacramental assistance that has been given to us abundantly, and the Scriptures provide a sound basis for optimism that we too can be faithful, and that when we fail we will be forgiven. How appropriate are those words of the Hail Mary, "pray for us now and at the hour of our death. Amen! "

Day 7 of Week 9: Application of the Senses
Christ was tempted by the enemy three times.

APPLICATION OF THE SENSES to the scriptural passages cited in Day 6 of this week, with special attention to the Two Leaders and the Two Strategies of Days 1 through 5.

The Windhover

To Christ our Lord

I caught this morning morning's minion, king-
  dom of daylight's dauphin, dapple-dawn-drawn Falcon, in his riding
  Of the rolling level underneath him steady air, and striding
High there, how he rung upon the rein of a wimpling wing
In his ecstasy! then off, off forth on swing,
  As a skate's heel sweeps smooth on a bow-bend; the hurl and gliding
  Rebuffed the big wind. My heart in hiding
Stirred for a bird,—the achieve of, the mastery of the thing!

Brute beauty and valour and act, oh, air, pride, plume, here
  Buckle! AND the fire that breaks from thee then, a billion
Times told lovelier, more dangerous, O my chevalier!

No wonder of it: sheer plod makes plough down sillion
  Shine, and blue-bleak embers, ah my dear,
Fall, gall themselves, and gash gold-vermillion.

GERARD MANLEY HOPKINS, S.J.

Week 10: *The Mission Begins*

A Further Call to Adventure: We live in a world of startling contrasts and paradoxes. The created universe is built on such a grand scale that it is only comprehensible in a piecemeal way. Marvelous too is the dream of God to send his Son to become a man on Planet Earth with a magnificent mission, a kingdom to build by enlisting followers to share in this, the greatest adventure, the most fantastic mission in the universe. But paradoxically the means to accomplish that conquest are at once apparently the most prosaic and yet the most difficult imaginable: self conquest, the following of Christ, and the love of one's neighbor.

Guidance for the Remainder of Phase Two Prayer

From this time on through the remainder of the second phase of the Exercises it is important in the contemplations on the public life of Jesus to focus our prayer on the GRACE we beg for and on the COLLO- QUY. *The grace will always be to know Jesus more intimately, to love him more intensely and to follow Him more closely.* The colloquy in all the contemplations on the public life is the one described in the meditation on the Two Leaders and Two Strategies (sometimes called the Two Standards) [147] and repeated in the meditation on the Three Classes [156-57]. This directive is given in [159] and [160] of the *Exercises*. Thus, the colloquy appropriate for all the contemplations on the public life of Jesus is the fourfold or quadruple colloquy in which we beg the grace to be received under the Standard of Christ, first in the highest spiritual poverty, and even in actual poverty and insults, if that be God's will. For a further treatment of this matter see the little book, *Poverty of Spirit*, by Metz.

> Godspll
>] days
> ? by
> day

The "Pilgrim's" Attitude, My Own: In his autobiography we read how on his journey to Rome with his companions, Ignatius was visited very specially by God:

> After he [Ignatius] became a priest he had decided to spend a year without saying mass, preparing himself and begging Our Lady to deign to place him with her Son. One day, while still a few miles from Rome, he was praying in a Church and experienced such a change in his soul and saw so clearly that God the Father had placed him with His Son Christ that his mind could not doubt that God the Father had indeed placed him with His Son (O'Callaghan translation, p. 89).

The Gift I seek: I beg the Father to place me, as He placed Ignatius, with His Son so that being His companion I may know Him better, love Him more and be more faithful in my service of Him and of His people. I further beg that I may imitate Jesus in the highest poverty and in being able to bear insults and contempt, provided I can do this without sin on the part of another and without any offense to God.

Days 1 & 2 of Week 10: Matthew 3: 13–17; Mark 1: 9–11; Luke 3: 21–22
Contemplation on Our Lord's Baptism by John in the Jordan.

FOCUS: Jesus is clearly called forth by his Father [158]; and see No. 40 in [273]. Jesus, having pondered in his heart the mystery of the Fatherhood of God and the mission given to him by the Father, decides to leave Nazareth. I try to be present to him as he reaches this decision, shares it with his mother, makes his farewells and leaves behind all that has helped to form his human traits up to this time.

All four evangelists treat of the baptism of Jesus, each in his own way, because this event is so important theologically. How grateful are you that as a baptized Christian you share in this anointing by the holy Spirit for your mission; that you are part of that new people of Israel; and that Jesus has taken upon himself the decisive judgment of God? What greater evidence of God's love for you could you seek? Do these great gifts also mean that, although not innocent, you may have a share to some degree in the role of suffering servant? Are you at this stage in your relationship with Jesus willing to have some such share in the hardships of the mission?

As you contemplate this scene, and if you experience an upwelling of gratitude, let it result in a COLLOQUY with each of the persons of the Trinity and with Mary, the mother of Jesus. Do not fail to discuss your possible share in the sufferings and hardships that may be part of your adventure in carrying out your part in the mission of Jesus.

Day 3 of Week 10: John 1: 19-39
"Behold, the Lamb of God, who takes away the sin of the world."

This section of the Gospel of John the Evangelist immediately following the Prologue is first of all concerned with John the Baptist's testimony to himself and to his mission; secondly with the Baptist's testimony to Jesus and his mission; and finally the decision by two of John the Baptist's disciples to become followers of Jesus, based on their master's remark, "Behold, the Lamb of God." The Baptist identifies his role by applying to himself the prophetic passage: "A voice cries out: In the desert prepare the way of the Lord! Make straight in the wasteland a highway for our God!" (Is 40: 3). Thus the words of Isaiah underscore John's awareness that his complete significance is in his relationship to Jesus.

Let us pray for the transparency of John the Baptist's witness to Jesus' mission in our own lives and work. We may apply to ourselves those words of Jesus spoken to his disciples, "You have not chosen me; I have chosen you."

Day 4 of Week 10: Repetition
"This is my beloved Son, with Whom I am well pleased."

Let this be a return to the most meaningful aspects of the baptism of Jesus and/or of the account of John the Baptist and his relationship to Jesus. At the moment of his baptism by John a heavenly voice confirms His sonship and his mission (Mt 3: 17).

Day 5 of Week 10: John 1: 19–39
Application of the Senses to John's "Witness."

Transport yourself in imagination to the scene in John's first chapter and become a witness to and a participant in what is going on and what is being said. What was so convincing about John the Baptist's testimony that prompted two of his disciples to become followers of Jesus? Speak to them and find out what moved them so.

Days 6 and 7 of Week 10: Teilhard de Chardin on Sanctifying Action
Our environment (milieu) is that of spirit, our life's goal is that His Kingdom may come.

These thoughts from *The Divine Milieu* are developed in Part One: "The Divinisation of our Activities." See "The Christian Problem of the Sanctification of Action" (Section 1, pp.50-53) and "The Final Solution: All Endeavor Cooperates to Complete the World in Christo Jesu" (Section 3, pp. 56-73).

The main idea that Teilhard presents here is what St. Paul presented initially—that every human life must in some fashion become a life in common with the life of Christ. Paul summed it up: "Whatever you do, do it in the name of our Lord Jesus Christ." Teilhard says right in the beginning that nothing is more certain, dogmatically, than that human action can be sanctified. The question that often plagues the person who values religion highly is: "How can one who believes in heaven and the Cross go on believing seriously in the value of worldly occupations?" Teilhard unhesitatingly insists that we can provide mutual nourishment for the love of God and a healthy love of the world by striving for a cleansing of our intention, a certain laudable detachment on the one hand, and toward the enrichment of our human lives on the other.

Elsewhere Teilhard addresses the same idea in different terms, namely that each of us is privileged to participate in forming the divine milieu, the environment of the Spirit in the world, not by withdrawing from the activities of the world but by immersing ourselves in them and excelling in them. We are empowered by the Creator of the Universe to share in "creating" the noosphere that is in the process of becoming. Teilhard comes back to one of his favorite themes, namely that the mystic (one who seeks the Spirit) should strive for achievement, to be as action oriented as the children of earth in their passion for progress. In a beautiful colloquy at the end of the passages referred to above, Teilhard prays that Our Lord will show his faithful ones just how their works will follow them into his kingdom.

In this poem written in 1882, Hopkins expresses eloquently that everything and everyone proclaims a special mission for which each one of us came onto the earth. The graced person, moreover, "acts" and "plays" Christ:

As kingfishers catch fire, dragonflies draw flame;
As tumbled over rim in roundy wells
Stones ring; like each tucked string, tells, each hung bell's
Bow swung finds tongue to fling out broad its name;
Each mortal thing does one thing and the same:
Deals out that being indoors each one dwells;
Selves—goes itself; myself it speaks and spells,
Crying "Whát I dó is me: for that I came."

I say móre: the just man justices;
Keeps grace: thát keeps all his goings graces;
Acts in God's eye what in God's eye he is—
Christ—for Christ plays in ten thousand places,
Lovely in limbs, and lovely in eyes not his
To the Father through the features of men's faces.

GERARD MANLEY HOPKINS, S.J.

Week 11: *Jesus Calls Me By Name*

Each one of us can and ought to find Jesus in those with whom we come in contact. This we know from the words of Jesus, "As long as you did it to the least of these, you did it to me." Conversely, is it easy for others to find Christ in me? Does the sign that Jesus set up as the means of recognizing his disciples, characterize me as having learned the lessons of life from Jesus? "By this shall all know that you are my disciples if you have love one for another." Could I be convicted on the basis of circumstantial evidence of being a Christian by one who otherwise knows nothing about me?

The Setting: In the Gospels there are a number of persons whom Jesus explicitly calls by name. Contemplating these mysteries we hear our own name called and we try to discover what happens within us at the sound of His voice.

The Gift I seek: I beg the Father to draw me to his Son, so that hearing Jesus call my name, as He invites me to a life of high adventure, I may better understand Him, experience more intensely His love for me and desire more ardently to serve Him and His people, and this in the highest poverty and contempt if that be His will.

Day 1 of Week 11: Luke 19: 1–10
"Zaccheus, come down quickly, for today I must stay at your house."

In this encounter with Jesus, Zacchaeus felt himself called to a whole new life. Now I climb the sycamore tree and ponder my own call as Jesus calls me by name and invites himself to stay at my house. What similarities can I see between Zacchaeus' dispositions and my own? Let me be grateful that by baptism and the other sacraments I have already been included in the New Israel. I pray that Jesus may find in me those qualities and dispositions that prompted him to seek out hospitality with Zacchaeus. I pray also for the kind of outlook that Jesus has with respect to sinners, and his flexibility in leaving aside other plans in favor of seeking out the sheep that is lost. As I hasten down from the sycamore tree and go with Jesus to my home, what do I want to say to Jesus? Will I talk to him about my hopes and plans for developing a more meaningful long term relationship with him and other members of his flock? Jesus calls me by name so that he may not only come to my home but may enter into the very fiber of my person and my life.

Day 2 of Week 11: Matthew 16: 13–18, 23
"You are Peter [rock], and upon this rock I will build my Church."

Jesus called Simon by a new name. This call was a great gift and it made clear Simon's role among the followers of Christ, the rock on which the community of Christians would be founded (see also Mk 8: 27–30; Lk 9: 18–21). But he still needed redemption. Jesus had to give him another name. Perhaps I can discover God's name for me. What is my role among His followers? Do I still need redemption? What does it mean to be called and in reality to be a "companion of Jesus"?

Jesus attempts to instruct Peter in God's mode of thinking as Jesus addresses him in terms that recall the rejection of Satan in the temptation account of Mt 4:10. Reflect what it may mean "to think as God does" in my own life. I will pray earnestly for the grace to think not as human beings do, but as God does.

I will pray to discover what name Jesus gives to me, perhaps, as he did with Peter, one name that describes my great worth to the Christian community and one that I can be proud of, and another that may tell of my weakness, but a name that I can discard when I am able to think like God does.

Day 3 of Week 11: A fantasy meditation
Jesus calls me by name.

In our Western culture the conferring of a name may be a casual routine nearly devoid of symbolism and of spiritual dimensions. It has long been a practice for the "Christian" name to be that of a saint. Sometimes one's birthday coincides with the feast day of a favorite saint, possibly also one's patron namesake. On other important occasions, such as at confirmation or on the occasion of making of vows, additional names are taken. In many cultures, such as those described in the Old and New Testaments, one's name, meant to inspire and to focus the one bearing it, commonly gave a clue to one's mission in life or accomplishments.

Do the Christian names that I bear, have special meaning for me? Do I have an affection for what the saint whose name I bear accomplished during life for the kingdom of God? By baptism I have received the special presence of the Holy Spirit, sent by the risen Messiah, to provide me with divine wisdom and divine love. In baptism I received the efficacious holy name of Jesus, and I have been anointed with the efficacious ointment of his name.

How well does the name Christian describe my attitudes? my lifestyle—including my relationships with others, both those dear to me and others in the wider community? How does "companion of

Jesus" describe my relationship to Jesus? Am I a companion of Jesus in any sense similar to that of his disciples who were attracted by him, and had their hopes and goals linked to his, as they understood them?

What names does Jesus give me that express my contributions to the Christian community that he founded? to the wider community of which I am a part? What names does Jesus confer on me, as he did on Peter (you satan), that reflect that I do not yet think like God in all aspects of my life?

I take my place among the disciples as they accompany Jesus to pray in solitude on the occasion of Peter's profession of faith in Jesus as the Messiah. The text, "Once when Jesus was praying in solitude, and the disciples were with him," furnishes the setting for joining them prayerfully. I speak, as my heart suggests that I should, with his disciples, and especially with Peter, asking that I may be taught the lessons that they learned at Jesus' feet, and from the Father. I ask Jesus to teach me how to think as God does as I prepare to embark on his mission.

Day 4 of Week 11: The Name of Jesus—the Jesus Prayer
"Nor is there any other name . . . by which we are to be saved."

A variation on the Jesus Prayer consists of a reverent repetition of the name of Jesus. It is efficacious inasmuch as Jesus becomes present as well as bringing salvation to the one praying, because Jesus "will save his people from their sins" (Mt 1: 21). Jesus is the Savior, as his name indicates, since "There is no salvation through anyone else, nor is there any other name under heaven given to the human race by which we are to be saved" (Acts 4: 12). His salvation today, as during his life on earth, consists in healing all our physical, spiritual and emotional disabilities, establishing peace with God, ourselves, and with all around us.

Speak the name of Jesus slowly, reverently and lovingly thus making Jesus present to yourself. Pause frequently yearning for Jesus' presence by which his gift of his salvation comes to you.

The author of the great Song of Songs, sublimely portraying the mutual love of the Lord and his people, has this to say about the divine name: "Your name spoken is a spreading perfume" (Song 1: 3). Apply this fragrant and healing name of Jesus to each of your senses and faculties until each is aglow with the presence and love of Our Savior.

Finally you may anoint others with the healing name of Jesus, by speaking or even thinking the name of Jesus over them. The most powerful and most consoling instrument for strengthening and healing yourself and others is the prayerful recitation of the holy name of Jesus. Whether you are in the presence of others or are at a distance from them when you anoint them with the name of Jesus matters not at all. When you walk along a busy street or across a crowded campus, you can silently anoint those whom you pass with the healing and strengthening fragrance of Jesus' name.

Day 5 of Week 11: John 11: 154
The raising of Lazarus—Jesus' greatest miracle.

Jesus called: "Lazarus, come out!" Lazarus heard himself called from death to life, from being bound to being free. Lying on the ledge in the tomb ponder your own little deaths and all that limits your freedom.

Spend some time reflecting on the human and divine drama that was being played out here as you read these passages in John. In particular, note the deeply felt human emotions of Jesus, his disciples, his other friends, and of his enemies. What does each episode mean to you personally in deepening your own spirituality? Do you yet have the love of friends or of God to lay down your life for your friend or friends, for your family, for your God? Pray to Jesus for insight into his love. Can you accept the fact that Jesus loves you as he did his Bethany friends. Jesus' gift of restored life to Lazarus was at the cost of offering up his own life. Lazarus, Mary, and Martha were his special friends but we may be sure that they represent everyman and everywoman who desires a deep and abiding friendship with Jesus.

Day 6 of Week 11: Repetition
Place yourself among the disciples called by our Lord.

Return to those parts of the meditations of Day 1 through Day 5 that have been most fruitful. Or, if you desire to meditate on new material I suggest the conversion of Saul, persecutor of the early Christians of Damascus, who was called Paul, and who became one of the great Apostles of the Church (Acts 9: 1-9).

Day 7 of Week 11: Application of the Senses
Place yourself so as to see and hear and be with Jesus.

In this exercise revisit scenes from the album of your fantasy and scriptural readings (Day 1 through Day 5). Place yourself in the scene upon which you are meditating and imagine as vividly as possible your participation in the discussion, or, if you prefer, take on less of a speaking and more of a listening role. Be sure, however, that you participate as appropriate in discussions with Jesus, his disciples, as well as with Mary and others. Imagine the scene more vividly; see the color of Zaccheus' tree, feel the texture of its bark; smell the dust in the air stirred up by the passersby and hear the sounds in each of the scenes.

In the process of more vividly experiencing the scene contemplated, it usually is easier to imagine your own response to Jesus. Or for instance, in the conversion of Saul, to experience gratitude for being struck down, blinded and raised up like Paul as Jesus' friend.

In the Acts of the Apostles (ch. 9-1), Luke describes Saul as "breathing murderous threats against the disciples of the Lord." From one of the most ardent persecutors of Jesus' little flock, he became one of the most zealous of the disciples and was ultimately reckoned as an apostle. Jesus took the persecution of his disciples personally, asking "Saul, Saul, why are you persecuting me?" (v.4) Saul's discernment of spirits was a very dramatic process and is described as a personal intervention by Jesus who pointed out what initial steps he must take to become his disciple. Jesus even goes so far as to communicate to Ananias that Saul "is a chosen instrument of mine to carry my name before Gentiles, kings and Israelites, and I will show him what he will have to suffer for my name" (9:15-16). The name Saul was exchanged for his new name Paul, a name that is synonymous with love of and apostolic zeal for the person of Jesus and the coming of his kingdom.

The Collar

I struck the board, and cried, "No more!
        I will abroad.
What? shall I ever sigh and pine?
My lines and life are free; free as the road,
Loose as the wind, as large as store.
  Shall I be still in suit?
 Have I no harvest but a thorn
To let me blood, and not restore
What I have lost with cordial fruit?
       Sure there was wine
Before my sighs did dry it, there was corn
  Before my tears did drown it.
Is the year only lost to me?
  Have I no bays to crown it?
No flowers, no garlands gay? all blasted?
      All wasted?
  Not so, my heart: but there was fruit,
     And thou hast hands.
  Recover all thy sigh-blown age
On double pleasures: leave thy cold dispute
Of what is fit, and not. Forsake thy cage,
     Thy rope of sands,
Which petty thoughts have made, and made to thee
  Good cable, to enforce and draw,
      And be thy law,
  While thou didst wink and wouldst not see.
      Away; take heed:
      I will abroad.
Call in thy death's head there; tie up thy fears.
      He that forbears
  To suit and serve his need,
      Deserves his load."
But as I raved and grew more fierce and wild
  At every word,
Methoughts I heard one calling, "Child!"
  And I replied, "My Lord."

GEORGE HERBERT

Week 12: *Jesus Teaches Me with Words of "Power and Light"*

My Attitude: The manifesto of the Kingdom is expressed in the Sermon on the Mount. Listening reverently to this discourse I allow the seed of Jesus' word to be implanted in me and take root. "Your Words, O Lord, are Power and Light!"

The Gift that I want and desire: I beg the Father to draw me to Jesus so that hearing his word I may receive it, receiving His word I may live it, and may more ardently desire to serve Him and His people in the highest poverty and contempt if that be His will.

Introduction to Making a Choice of a State or Way of Life

Guidelines for making a choice or in coming to a decision as well as a discussion of the subject matter about which a choice should be made are presented in the text of the *Exercises* [169-174]. The guiding principle is that "only one thing is really important—to seek and find what God calls me to at this time in my life" [169].

Hugo Rahner provides an important insight concerning the "Election," as such choices have traditionally been called, in his comment: "During the exercises of the Election, the exercitant should not direct his attention simply to the movement of spirits going on within him (that is by discerning the fluctuations of consolation and desolation), but rather to the love of God which both precedes and accompanies all movements of the soul—and he will do this by continuing to contemplate the mysteries of the life of Christ" (p. 146).

Day 1 of Week 12: Matthew 5: 1-48
"He went up the mountain. . .his disciples came to him. He began to teach them."

Mountains are metaphors for the meeting place between God and his people. Many times in the Gospels we are told that Jesus went up to the mountain to pray, a favorite setting for his prayer. Should you not, as well? In the presence of God listen to the words of Jesus, letting their power and his person transform you.

"The central message of Jesus' preaching is the coming of the kingdom of heaven and the need for repentance, a complete change of heart and conduct, on the part of those who receive this great gift of God" (NAB, introduction to and commentary on Matthew, p. 3).

The introductory segment of Matthew's fifth chapter designates

those who are blessed (vv. 3-12), a phrase used in the Wisdom litera-
ture and in the Psalms; the role of his followers as expressed by their
deeds (vv. 13-16); and Jesus' position as regards the Mosaic law (vv.
17-20). The next major segment (vv. 21-48), consisting of six examples
of the conduct required of his disciples, contrasts the holiness or righteousness of the scribes, experts in interpreting the Old Testament
law, and the more acceptable holiness of the followers of Jesus.

Ignatius uses the term "Election" to mean what today we refer to
as "making a choice" about something important in our lives,
whether it relates to selecting a long term career or way of life, or
whether it relates to choices within a commitment to a way of life already chosen. The Election properly arrived at is informed by the
wisdom and love of the Holy Spirit and is strengthened by motivation derived from contemplation of the life of Christ. In accord with
those of Ignatius in the *Exercises*, guidelines are presented below to
assist in making whatever election or major choices are in order. I em-
phasize that you must not feel that an election is required of you.
However, it is important that in the discernment process you should
take note of whether or not you may be called to make some kind of
election either to a new kind of life or to some change in the form of
life to which you are already called.

Begin with a segment from this extended "Sermon on the
Mount," such as the Beatitudes, or the Similes of Salt and Light and
read them slowly and meditatively. Reflect on the meaning in terms
of your personal relationship to Jesus as his disciple. Then read reflec-
tively the following guidelines from the *Exercises* [175-89]. Pray for
guidance of the Spirit and increased motivation inspired by the en-
thusiastic example of Jesus as he carries out his ministry (Mt. 5: 1-48).

Day 2 of Week 12: Repetition
"He began to teach them."

Return to the Scriptural passage in Matthew (5: 1-48) and to the
Guidelines for an Election, going from one to the other to the extent
that this is spiritually nourishing. Pray for guidance from Jesus as you
seek a closer personal relationship that will grow out of your closer
following of the will of God as you come to recognize it.

Day 3 of Week 12: Repetition
"And great crowds ... followed ... him. ... and, his disciples."

Return to the most fruitful considerations, prayers for guidance,
and colloquys that spontaneously develop as you seek to find your
place in the great adventure of discipleship of the Lord. Place your-

self in each of several scenes depicted in the "Sermon on the Mount" using each of your sense faculties. Additionally, if applicable, consider the Guidelines from the *Exercises* detailed under the captions below:

THREE TIMES OR SITUATIONS WHEN A CORRECT AND GOOD CHOICE OF A STATE OR WAY OF LIFE MAY BE MADE [175–88M].

SOME DIRECTIONS FOR THE RENEWAL OF OR RECOMMITMENT TO A STATE OR WAY OF LIFE ALREADY CHOSEN [189].

Day 4 of Week 12: Matthew 6: 1–34
"When you pray, go to your inner room. . .and pray to your Father in secret."

Meditate on those parts of this section of the Sermon and in particular reflect on those aspects that relate to decisions, both great and small, that are related to your Election. Give special attention to the meaning of the Lord's Prayer in your life and in your Election. The concept of becoming a "contemplative in action," which Ignatius proposed for his extended Jesuit family, takes on a fresh meaning in post-Vatican II times as the laity develop a personalized Ignatian spirituality.

Weave into your meditation, as appropriate, considerations from Guidelines that relate to the Election [169, 175-189].

Day 5 of Week 12: Matthew 14: 22-33
Bid me come to you on the water, Lord.

Often in the first burst of enthusiasm we are very brave, perhaps even improvident or foolhardy, though well intentioned. Afterward when we come to realize the importance of what we are called to do, or when we become overwhelmed with the thought "I can't believe that I am walking safely on the water," we falter. Then we need to remember the words of Jesus to Peter, or perhaps turn them into a prayer: "Lord, help my unbelief; give me courage not to doubt but to believe." "Take courage, it is I; do not be afraid." The phrase, "it is I" must have inspired Peter with confidence and should do so with us, because it has a time honored meaning that Jesus in saying it, shares in the divine power to save (Ps 18: 17-18; 144: 7; Exod 3: 14; Is 43: 10; 51: 12).

How appropriate is "The Soul's Lament" by Teilhard de Chardin (*Writings in Time of War*, "Cosmic Life," pp. 43-45). Here Teilhard expresses the doubt and anguish that every one experiences who has sacrificed and saved to buy the pearl of great price—marriage, family, scholarship, religious life, etc.—wondering later if it really was a great bargain or possibly a waste of time and effort. He voices similar concerns but a more positive point of view in *The Divine Milieu* ("Conclusion to Parts One and Two, The Meaning of the Cross," pp. 101-104).

Day 6 of Week 12: Matthew 7: 1–29
"Everyone who listens to these words of mine and acts on them will be like a wise man who built his house on a rock."

Meditate upon the person as well as upon the teachings of Jesus as he preaches to the people, outlining his path to holiness. Speak to him about what is required in your life by way of choices so as to circumvent the obstacles along the way. Keep in mind your objectives relating to the Election, with the importance of a personal relationship with Jesus being paramount. Share various experiences with Him as did the disciples and his other followers. Pray for a deep strengthening of your sense of conversion so that you may live for God, and that you may feel fulfilled thereby. Pray for the emergence of some specific and important choice that may have been only vaguely grasped previously, and pray for the courage to meet that choice with peace and strength.

Day 7 of Week 12: Repetition
"But seek first the kingdom [of God] and his righteousness."

Review the prayer of this week to discover how the Lord has been teaching you and whither the Spirit of God has been guiding you. Return to the most meaningful Scriptural passages from chapters 5, 6, 7, and 14 of Matthew and to the Guidelines for an Election, going from one to the other to the extent that this is spiritually energizing. Pray for guidance from Jesus as you seek a closer personal relationship that will grow out of your closer following of the will of God as you come to recognize it.

The Pillar of the Cloud

Lead, kindly Light, amid the encircling gloom,
                Lead thou me on;
The night is dark, and I am far from home,
                Lead thou me on.
Keep thou my feet: I do not ask to see
The distant scene: one step enough for me.

I was not ever thus, nor prayed that thou
                Shouldst lead me on;
I loved to choose and see my path; but now
                Lead thou me on.
I loved the garish day, and, spite of fears,
Pride ruled my will: remember not past years.

So long thy power hath blest me, sure it still
                Will lead me on,
O'er moor and fen, o'er crag and torrent, till
                The night is gone.
And with the morn those angel faces smile
Which I have loved long since, and lost a while.

                    JOHN HENRY NEWMAN

Week 13: *Jesus Heals Me*

My attitude: With hope, love, and faith I will be healed and so energized that I can do all that my Father wants of me. I realize also that the healing ministry of Jesus is a saving ministry as well. His concern is not just to restore the withered limb or the nonfunctioning organ to physical well-being, but that the one whom he heals may turn from his sin and believe in him. Entering into these mysteries in prayer, I present myself to Jesus as one in need of healing in body, mind and spirit.

What I want and desire: I beg the Father to draw me to Jesus so that in his presence my helplessness will be revealed and I can allow him to give me his healing love. With this experience of his love I ask for a more ardent desire to serve him and his people, even in highest poverty and contempt, if that be his will.

Day 1 of Week 13: Luke 11: 1–13
"Lord, teach us to pray!"

Let us now meditate for a short time on the story of the petition that gave rise to the Lord's prayer as recounted by Luke. "He [Jesus] was praying in a certain place, and when he had finished, one of his disciples said to him, 'Lord, teach us to pray, just as John taught his disciples.' He said to them, 'When you pray, say: Father, hallowed be your name, your kingdom come. Give us each day our daily bread and forgive us our sins, for we ourselves forgive everyone in debt to us, and do not subject us to the final test'" (Lk 11: 1-4). Each and every one of those phrases in the Lord's Prayer is a petition. The petition for forgiveness in the same measure as we forgive those who have wronged us, is a plea for healing of rifts. As we contemplate the Gospel scene reflect on the way that Jesus proceeds to provide deeper insight into how God looks upon the intensity with which we make our petition.

Try to imagine you hear Jesus saying those words to you that he spoke to his earlier disciples and ask yourself, "Do I hesitate to believe his words?" "Do I think they are really too good to be true?" "Do I really believe that Jesus will give me whatever I ask for?" "If I knock will the door be opened?" "If I seek will I find the answer?" Try to remember that Jesus seems to look for intensity of desire in his response to prayerful petition. As you arrive at answers to these questions share your thoughts and desires with Jesus.

Day 2 of Week 13: John 5: 1–9
Yes, Lord, I want to be well. I want to be healed!

Jesus' question to this sick and crippled man is addressed also to me. "Do you want to be well?" I show the Lord my need for healing: my pettiness, my pride, my ambition, my need for security and control, my disordered passions, my self-deception. The paralytic had been crippled for thirty-eight years, and nearly despaired of a cure. What was it that prompted Jesus to select this paralytic from the "large number of ill, blind, lame, and crippled"? John repeatedly stressed Jesus' ability to read hearts, meaning that he recognized genuine faith. Now I too say, "Yes, Lord, I want to be healed."

Day 3 of Week 13: Repetition
"And I tell you, ask and you will receive."

Return to those aspects of Days 1 and 2 of this week that have been most helpful in recognizing God's love expressed so richly in the mysteries of the life of Jesus, our incarnate God. Pay special attention to those aspects of your life and activities in which the love of Jesus may be said to have exercised its healing in you.

Day 4 of Week 13: Application of the Senses
"Give us each day our daily bread and forgive us our sins."

In the light of your meditation experience of Day 3, place yourself again in the scenes of Day 1 and/or Day 2. Pay special attention to recognizing God's love as it is expressed in these mysteries.

Day 5 of Week 13: Luke 18: 35–43
"Jesus, Son of David, have pity on me!"
                    "What do you want me to do for you?"

His approach to Jericho marks the final leg of Jesus' journey to Jerusalem and thus to his passion and death. This story summarizes all of Jesus' ministry as well as the opposition of others to that ministry (Lk 18: 39; 19: 7). Those in front of this beggar try to keep him from making himself a nuisance to Jesus. But Jesus not only heard him but, because of his exquisite discernment of hearts, "Jesus stopped and ordered that he be brought to him." Twice Luke has made it clear that Jesus' ministry is to bring sight to the blind, as fulfillment of God's promises. Twice also Luke indicates that one should invite the poor, the lame, and the blind to share one's banquet.

What consolation it should be for those many persons in every society who are born blind or who become blind, or ill, or lame or disabled to realize, as Luke did in a special way, the great love and esteem that Jesus has for them. I know from experience that more than one person in my retreat who literally became blind after many years of sight, came to realize that only when they had lost their vision, did they have the kind of insight that is a true gift of God. Luke also points out the blindness of the disciples, who lacked persistence and faith, compared to the blind beggar (18: 31-34). Reflect on the depth of your own faith and the level of your persistence. What is your response to Jesus' question to you, "What do you want me to do for you?" Pray that you may be filled with a great urgency, growing out of your response to Jesus' love, that would prompt you to cry out insistently, "Jesus, Son of David, have pity on me!"

Day 6 of Week 13: See de Mello (pp.119-20)
Jesus approaches us lovingly and humbly.

This devotional exercise may help you to experience the love of Christ for you. It was a favorite exercise of Saint Teresa of Avila. Many find it difficult to believe that Jesus loves them unconditionally. At first, you too may have difficulty with the fact that he approaches you humbly. Jesus wants our love and knows the difficulties that we have in the face of power—it very commonly drives out love and makes us look to our own protection. This exercise basically consists in imagining that you see Jesus standing before you looking at you lovingly and humbly. Note the emotions that well up in you as you observe Jesus' attitude toward you. Just allow yourself to be loved.

Day 7 of Week 13: Repetition
Return to what best elicits a generous response to God's will.

Because of the rich source of material for meditation and contemplation throughout the preceding days, return to those parts that are most fruitful in eliciting your generosity in terms of the Election. There should be both a constant awareness and "emphasis that any Election made by discerning the fluctuations of consolation and desolation must always be formed and guided by the continued prayerful contemplation of the mysteries of Christ's life on earth" (Rahner, pp. 144–45). The process of Ignatian discernment, culminating in the Election, is thoroughly Christological, inasmuch as it is carried through by the contemplation of Jesus' earthly history.

Because consolation and desolation are terms that Ignatius uses and whose understanding is fundamental to discernment they are carefully described in Guidelines of the *Exercises* [316–17].

The Face of Christ

The tragic beauty of the face of Christ
shines in the face of man;

the abandoned old live on
in shabby rooms, far from inner comfort.
Outside, in the street
din and purpose, the world like a fiery animal
reined in by youth. Within
a pallid tiring heart
shuffles about its dwelling.

Nothing, or so little, come of life's promise.
Out of broken men, despised minds
what does one make—
a roadside show, a graveyard of the heart?

The Christian God reproves
faithless ranting minds
crushing like upper and lower stones
Christ, fowler of street and hedgerow
of cripples and the distempered old
—eyes blind as woodknots,
tongues tight as immigrants—
takes in His gospel net
all the hue and cry of existence.

Heaven, of such imperfection,
wary, ravaged, wild?

Yes. Compel them in.

DANIEL BERRIGAN, S.J.

Week 14: *Jesus Challenges Me*

Consider again the challenging words of the official 1983 Jesuit assembly in Rome which summed up the situation encountered by modern men and women practicing the fundamentals of Christianity and attempting to develop a personally pervasive spirituality—that is, those wanting to be contemplatives in action.

> Our contemplation of the world reveals a situation frequently hostile to the spreading of the Kingdom. The dominant ideologies and systems—political, economic, social and cultural—often prevent an adequate response to the most elementary aspirations of the human family at both national and international levels. A pervasive materialism and the worship of human autonomy obscure or obliterate concern for the things of God, leaving the minds and hearts of many of our contemporaries cold and empty. This both reveals and causes a profound crisis of faith that expresses itself in an atheism at once theoretical, practical and institutional. Lack of respect for a loving Creator leads to a denial of the dignity of the human person and the wanton destruction of the environment. Massive poverty and hunger, brutal oppression and discrimination, a frightening arms race and the nuclear threat: all offer evidence of sin in human hearts and in the core of contemporary society. (*Documents of the 33rd General Congregation of the Society of Jesus*, p. 56)

My perception and attitude: Of the King's followers much will be asked. There will be the "one thing necessary" for an adequate following of our Lord; but for the generous follower of Jesus desiring to offer distinguished service there will be the "one thing more." Pondering the challenges, I look to see what movements are taking place within me.

What I want and desire: I beg the Father to draw me to Jesus so that I may hear and understand the challenge to which He calls me, thrill to the high adventure that stirs my being and ardently desire to serve Him and His people, sharing His lot and His suffering.

Day 1 of Week 14: Luke 18: 35–43
"Jesus, Son of David, have pity on me!"

A **Fantasy Exercise:** Last week on Day 5 you contemplated this moving encounter between Jesus and the blind Bartimaeus. Today return to deepen this experience by an APPLICATION OF THE SENSES. Take the place of the blind beggar and relive his experience as thoroughly as possible. Fill out the story in fantasy as you take on the identity of the "insignificant" beggar on the roadside in Jericho. Keep in mind that the exercise is designed to increase your generous response to Jesus as you come to appreciate the special love that prompts the Good Shepherd to single you out for the cure of your blindness. Take your place as the blind person sitting by the dusty, hot, unpaved road begging. As a beggar you depend on the gifts of others, often grudgingly given, as your only source of sustenance. You are basically an outcast without any socially redeeming qualities. Where did you sleep last night? How did you find your way to the roadside this morning to take up your suppliant's position? As they go by, what do people say to you, if they say anything at all to recognize your common humanity? As they give to you, do they try to cheer you or do they contribute while wishing you did not exist?

All at once you hear the scurrying of many feet, and you cough from the cloud of dust that they stir up. You hear the clamor of excited voices. "What is happening?" you ask, and they tell you, "Jesus of Nazareth is passing by." A desperate surge of excitement seizes you as you recognize that here is the one chance in your lifetime to regain your sight. Though you are blind, you have grown up hearing and relishing the Scriptures that promised the Messiah, and you never forgot that the Messiah would be of the house of David and that he would bring salvation to his people.

Upon hearing this hopeful news you jump to your feet and shout, "Jesus, Son of David, have pity on me." But the people walking in front of you try to hush you; they tell you to stop making a nuisance of yourself. But nothing and no one is going to deprive you of this one great opportunity. All of a sudden, Jesus hears you, turns and asks that you be brought to him! This is indeed your great opportunity!

What is your conversation, your colloquy with Jesus now as he asks you "What do you want me to do for you?" It sounds as if Jesus may give you anything you want—as he did with Solomon, who asked to be given wisdom. "Lord, please let me see." Perhaps Jesus answers, "I know that you have been blind a long time, but I have blessed you with a different kind of vision—insight. As a result of this gift you have recognized me as your Savior. I say to you as I said to Bartimaeus long ago, 'Have sight; your faith has saved you.'" Speak freely to your Savior and hear what he wants to say to you as he gazes on you lovingly and humbly.

As you begin to follow Jesus does he tell you that Jericho was his last stop before going to Jerusalem for his passion and death? Are you prepared to follow Jesus to Jerusalem and stick with him through those terrible days? Does your insight into the Scriptures tell you that Jesus, Son of David, would suffer, die and rise again? And when Jesus asks you, "are you willing to give up your life, if necessary, in exchange for your sight?" Do you not say, "No, Lord, that I could not do; however, I am ready to give my life in exchange for the opportunity to follow you, because you have saved me through my God-given faith. I will follow you anywhere that you lead me!" And where does he lead you?

Day 2 of Week 14: Luke 10: 25–37
"Who is my neighbor?"

This scriptural text is from the first part of Luke's travel narrative of Jesus' final journey to Jerusalem. It contains Jesus' instruction on the meaning of the Christian Way, dealing as it does with numerous lessons on the nature and demands of being his disciple (Lk 9: 51-62; 13: 21-30). This narrative first provides a dramatic lesson on mercy toward the needy, and then sets forth the startling observation that non-Jews in observing the law may enter into eternal life. We may assume that the lawyer had listened to what Jesus had said about Christian mission and tested Jesus with his question (Lk 10: 25). But in his story of the good Samaritan Jesus demonstrates that love is superior to legalism.

Jesus' story implies that there is no one who is not my neighbor. The challenge here is to live up to the demands of complete discipleship in terms of love of neighbor in active service and love of Jesus in prayer. In meditating on this dramatic story let us pray that we may fulfil the law written in our hearts and in our minds: "You shall love the Lord, your God, with all your heart, with all your being, with all your strength, and with all your mind, and your neighbor as Yourself" (Lk 10: 27).

Day 3 of Week 14: Luke 10: 38–42
"There is need of only one thing!"

These verses are devoted by Luke to two themes, first that it is important for the disciples to hear the words of Jesus the teacher; and secondly that Jesus is concerned about women and includes them among his close friends and disciples. Luke is at pains to point out that Jesus acted contrary to Jewish cultural norms in three respects: "Jesus is alone with women who are not his relatives; a woman serves him at table; and Jesus is teaching a woman in her own house" (NJBC, Karris, p. 702). Luke underscores the importance to the early church of "household" Christianity since women hosted the church in their houses. The phrase, "Mary sat beside the Lord at his feet listening to him speak," is remarkable for the fact that in the first-century Judaism of Palestine a woman would assume the posture of a "disciple at the master's feet" (Lk 10: 39). The point is that listening to the word of Jesus is the underpinning of all discipleship—the uniquely important, as well as the best part (Lk 8: 35; Acts 22: 3).

This story of Martha and Mary follows on the story of the Good Samaritan, in which Jesus praised the Samaritan's practical service. One may infer that "the whole gospel is not contained in loving service to others, no matter how important that is. There must be time to listen to his word—devotion to Jesus is the one thing required (Lk 10: 39-42). This relationship shows itself in loving service, but without prayer, care for others' needs may not be love" (CBC, Kodell, p. 957). The challenge to the companion of Jesus is to be a combination of both Martha and Mary (the sisters of Lazarus), to be the contemplative in action whose work for the Lord is animated by constant intimacy with Him. I will pray for the kind of abiding friendship with Jesus that will enrich my life and that of my neighbor.

Day 4 of Week 14: Repetition
Recognizing God's love in the mysteries of Jesus' life.

I will return to those scenes and aspects of previous days of this week that have been most helpful in the discernment process and especially in recognizing God's love expressed so richly in the mysteries of the life of Jesus, my incarnate God who became a human being for love of me and my fellow human beings.

Day 5 of Week 14: Mark 10: 17–31
"Go, sell what you have, and give to [the] poor. . . . Then come, [and] follow me."

This passage in Mark's narrative consists of three parts dealing with wealth and the kingdom: 1) the story of the rich man (vv. 17-22); 2) Jesus' instructional commentary to his disciples (vv. 23-27); and 3) his teaching about the rewards for those who forego riches (vv. 28-31). The main points are that wealth can be a hindrance to discipleship and that the rewards of following Jesus are greater than the sacrifices.

The initial, inauspicious exchange between the rich young man who ran up and knelt down before him and the seemingly testy response of Jesus (Mk 10: 18-19) gave way quickly to the heartwarming scene, "Jesus, looking at him, loved him." The private instruction of Jesus to his disciples following the public teaching episode involving the saddened rich man, was possibly prompted by their amazement at Jesus' statement to the rich man. It was difficult for them to adjust to the idea that renunciation of wealth could have beneficial results.

Reflect meditatively on these passages and apply their lessons to yourself, especially in light of the Election choice that you may have made or that you may feel called to make. How generous are you genuinely impelled to be in response to the opportunity to share in the adventurous work of the kingdom? Speak to the disciples about their "elections." What were the deciding factors in the decisions of those with whom you speak? As you feel moved to speak to each of the members of the Trinity and to Mary, ask what discipleship looks like from their perspective. Does their response or reflections from meditating on the scene prompt you to colloquies to express your joy and your fears at being called to discipleship? Jesus challenges you with these words: "There is one thing more you must do." Listen now as He tells you in your own circumstances what one thing more is required of you.

Day 6 of Week 14: The Contemplative in Action
The "Morning Offering" fom the Hymn of the Universe.

King (1988, p. 102) says that of the questions that mystics have felt called upon to answer, "one concerns the relationship between contemplation and action; another, the place of quiet and passivity before the divine agent; and a third concerns the relationship of the mystic to society at large. All of these were central issues in the thought of Teilhard," and you have addressed some of these in the meditation on Martha and Mary earlier in this week of the Exercises.

The Jesuit tradition, to which Teilhard belonged, claims that contemplation is to be found in the activity itself. Teilhard concluded that if one could contemplate as one acted, the whole quality of the act would change. "To do ordinary things with a perception of their enormous value. This, I think, is the mysticism that is to come" (King, p. 103). The mysticism of Teilhard is based on the perception that human work has great value—the mysticism of every day life. Teilhard, in common with other mystics, speaks of a special way of seeing. He wrote The Divine Milieu as a "way of teaching how to see."

Our "vision" of the universe over the past several decades has undergone a startlingly rapid development. We now know that the universe is formed of galaxies that are billions of light years apart and they are at least 15 to 20 billion years old. But Teilhard has identified the problem that arises: "A crisis of vision afflicts our present time. We seem to have seen too much and we are left with 'a feeling of futility, of being crushed by the enormities of the cosmos; we lose our taste for action" (King, p. 105). Teilhard's vision helps us to see that through our activity "the universe is becoming personalized in Christ and we experience a sublime happiness because of the central role we play in the cosmic process" (King, p. 112). Teilhard has helped us to see that we can do ordinary deeds as acts of love.

This is basically what the "Morning Offering" as a devotion to the Sacred Heart of Jesus has fostered over the past hundred years. Christ is recognized as the goal of all of the Christian's activity, since, whatever the Christian does, it is to Christ to whom it is done. Thus one begins to live in union with Jesus. Such considerations are important to mysticism that works to build the Body of Christ. This is contemplation in action that is directed to building the earth, and, as a result activity and contemplation become united and full of vitality as the contemplative in action engages life in all its fullness.

Using the Second or Third Method of Praying, outlined in the "Introduction to the Retreat," under "Ignatian Methods of Praying," meditate on the meaning of each word or phrase in either the traditional formula of the "Morning Offering" or in your own prayer by which you offer to God the fruits of the harvest which your day will bring. A most moving "Morning offering" is that of Teilhard de Chardin in "The Mass on the World" in the *Hymn of the Universe*. Remember that formulated prayers are composed to be a help to petition and to contemplation. You may wish to formulate your own version of them as you become responsive to the Holy Spirit in time of prayer. This method will be very useful not only during this retreat but as you develop a deeper pattern of spirituality in your life after the retreat [245-57].

Day 7 of Week 14: Micah 6: 8
"You have been told, O man [and woman], what is good, and what the Lord requires of you."

In the presence of God I let these prophetic words take root within me: "You have been told, O man and woman, what is good and what the Lord requires of you: Only to do the right and to love goodness and to walk humbly with your God."

I will return to those scenes and topics of previous days of this week that have been most helpful in the discernment process and especially in recognizing God's love expressed so richly in the mysteries of the life of Jesus, my incarnate God who became a human being for love of me and my fellow human beings. I will dwell especially on those elements that inspire me to generosity in the Election and in my growth in becoming a contemplative in action!

Batter my heart, three-personed God, for you
    As yet but knock; breathe, shine, and seek to mend;
    That I may rise and stand, o'erthrow me and bend
Your force to break; blow, burn, and make me new.
I, like an usurped town to another due,
    Labour to admit you, but O, to no end.
    Reason, your viceroy in me, me should defend,
But is captived and proves weak or untrue.
Yet dearly I love you and would be loved fain,
    But am betrothed unto your enemy.
Divorce me, untie, or break that knot again,
    Take me to you, imprison me, for I,
    Except you enthrall me, never shall be free,
    Nor ever chaste except you ravish me.

JOHN DONNE

Week 15: *Jesus Nurtures Me*

Tired from healing the wounds of humanity by the Lake of Gennesaret, Jesus and his disciples seek some rest on the shore of the Mediterranean, only to be recognized and sought out by a Gentile woman whose insistent "great faith" not only prompts him to perform a cure, but changes the Father's timetable for bringing salvation to the Gentiles. Jesus knows intense discouragement too, as a result of opposition from the people of Israel. Nevertheless, he is able to put his own discouragement aside and, seeking out persons who give promise of faith, nurture each one according to need: "Come to me, all you who labor and are burdened, and I will give you rest. Take my yoke upon you and learn from me, for I am meek and humble of heart; and you will find rest for yourselves. For my yoke is easy, and my burden light" (Mt. 11: 28-30).

My situation and attitude: Hungry and exhausted, the Lord's followers cannot long continue in his service unless he gives them rest. I come into his presence to be refreshed with living water, strengthened with the bread of life, and invigorated by his holy word.

What I need and want: I beg the Father to draw me to Jesus so that I may become more aware of his passionate concern for me and accept his nurturing love. I want to be more passionate than ever before, in serving him and his people, sharing his lot in poverty and the contempt of others if that is his will.

Day 1 of Week 15: John 2: 1–11
"They have no wine. . . .Do whatever he tells you."

This is John's story of the first public appearance of Jesus and of the first of the signs that he performed, the first disclosure of the mystery of his Incarnation. Mary, here designated only as the mother of Jesus, symbolizes the ideal disciple of Jesus. Jesus' observation, "My hour is not yet come," appears to allude to Jesus' Passion and resurrection, which John consistently refers to as "his hour" (7: 30; 8: 20; 13: 1; 17: 1). How appropriate to reflect on "my hour"—our own hour, the hour of our death at which time all of us will discover who we really are. Throughout our lives we are constantly becoming, we are constantly growing, but we do not know who we really are and who we will become in the kingdom of God after our own passion and death—only God knows.

As we contemplate this most moving passage of John's Gospel let us respond in colloquies, praying that we may each discover who we are and, to at least some degree, who we are to become. It is our goal not only to put on Christ, but to become Christ, so to speak, for the microcosm in which each of us lives. Ignatius' main concern in contemplating the life of Christ is always the cross, whose special meaning for us is that the life of Christ is more than an inspiring example. It is "the fundamental theological principle behind all Christian spiritual life, which is ultimately nothing more nor less than the conforming of one's whole being through grace with the crucified and risen Lord of glory" (Rahner, p. 99).

Day 2 of Week 15: Repetition
To know the Lord better in order to love him more intensely.

Because of the Christological importance of the account of the Wedding at Cana and its rich incarnational symbolism, I return there with Jesus, Mary, and the disciples and I contemplate again this scene, looking at it from the point of view of the Incarnation. As I pray during this second phase of the Exercises "to know the Lord better in order to love him more intensely and follow him more faithfully," I basically pray for the gift to be not just a spectator or an outsider. But I ask for the grace to be true to myself by being present to the mystery of Incarnation as manifested in Cana in this commonplace but most important celebration.

Day 3 of Week 15: Matthew 15: 21–28 & Mark 7: 24–30
"Woman, great is your faith. Let it be done for you as you wish."

This episode takes place on the Mediterranean coast where Jesus apparently went for rest and seclusion (Mk 7: 24) since, as illustrated earlier in the previous scene at Gennesaret, the crowds had nearly worn him out (Mk 6: 53-56). Matthew is mainly interested in the universality of Jesus' mission. Matthew refers to the woman, a Greek, as a Canaanite, and, therefore, a Gentile, yet one who knew enough about Jesus to call out, "Have pity on me, Lord, Son of David! My daughter is tormented by a demon." She came and fell at Jesus' feet, diligently seeking a cure for her daughter. Jesus explained his silence by pointing out that he should not exceed his divine mandate (Mt 15: 24). But the woman was so persistent that Jesus then publicly recognized her "great faith" and praised her generously. He indicated that such faith advanced the timetable for his mission to the Gentiles. Then he granted her wish and her daughter was instantly healed.

The message in both Matthew and Mark is clear—intense desire, reverent and insistent prayer based on great faith in Jesus, Son of

David, and Lord, prompts Jesus to grant her prayer, "Let it be done for you as you wish" (Mt 15: 28). Teilhard de Chardin's concept that each of us can perform work that is of cosmic importance takes on greater plausibility in the light of this Gentile woman's success in changing the time frame in which the Father would have his Son carry his message to the Gentiles. What she has done, each of us can do, if our faith is as great as hers. What do I have to do—what do I have to become in order to have such faith?

Day 4 of Week 15: John 4: 4–42
"I am he [the Messiah] the one who is speaking with you."

Samaritans and Samaria play a significant role in the gospels of Luke and John. This passage has a threefold division: (1) the much-loved story of an anonymous woman at Jacob's well whose growth in faith in Jesus took place without any of the "signs" that he had performed earlier (4: 4-30); (2) a discussion between Jesus and his disconcerted disciples that developed into an instruction on the nature of missionary activity and its rewards (4: 31-38); and (3) the coming to faith in Jesus by the Samaritan townspeople (4: 39-42).

John's main interest in the two days' stay of Jesus in Samaria is his revelation of himself as "Messiah" to the woman and as "Savior of the world" to the townsfolk. Once again Jesus reveals himself and the message of his Father to the most unlikely people, to those who are regarded as the most "unworthy." But what are the criteria by which the Father chooses those whom he seeks out? Faith, responsiveness to and a capacity for growth in faith, and an intensity of desire seem to be characteristic of all those to whom Jesus reveals himself and his mission.

Let us, as we contemplate these beautifully elaborated scenes full of divine and human emotion, pray to the Father to seek us out, to deepen our faith, and fan the intensity of our desire to drink from the fountain of living water. As we lift up our eyes and take a look at the fields white with harvest, may we have insight to see as Jesus sees, to be able to read hearts, and to think as God thinks!

Day 5 of Week 15: John 4: 4–42
Return to the well in the Samaritan town.

I return to this heartwarming scene, so full of meaning for those who would be disciples of Jesus. In this Repetition, I again place myself as a participant in the event and the dialogue; I respond in conversation or colloquy as I feel moved to do so. I hear and relish the words of Jesus that have special meaning in my life as a disciple in his harvest fields. I pray for those qualities that are the object of God's special seeking in those that he draws to himself.

Day 6 of Week 15: Matthew 11: 25–30
"Learn from me, for I am meek and humble of heart."

This passage is part of the narrative section of the third book of Matthew that deals with the groundswell of opposition to Jesus because of his teaching (11: 2-24; 12: 1-50). The hostility toward him had been repeatedly manifested (3: 10–13: 34; 8: 10; 9: 1–13), with much of the rejection coming from the Pharisees, who eventually began to plot Jesus' death (12: 14, 30–36). The previous passages are depressing because sadly they record the ingratitude and lack of repentance on the part of people in the towns where Jesus had expended so much effort.

Longing for companionship and intimacy, I welcome this invitation of Jesus to share His rest as He shares my burden. I ardently desire to give myself totally to the love and service of Jesus and his people. In Jesus is God's wisdom. By attempting to model my life and my thinking on Jesus, I pray that the Son may wish to reveal his Father to me. May I learn to take up his yoke and become meek and humble of heart, and so become able to personify Jesus to those whom I am privileged to serve.

Day 7 of Week 15: Repetition
Place me again with Jesus in the small towns of Palestine.

I return to the rich lessons of this week, attempting to become a participant in the dialogue by means of discussion and colloquy. I will make the scenes vivid by application of the sense faculties. But most of all I will attempt to act and react to Jesus as I would to a friend, to one who loves me sincerely and who wants me to share his wisdom, his yoke, his burdens, and his rest. I will imagine those who are my best and truest friends and see if I can converse with Jesus as I do with them. If not, perhaps I may need to examine whether my image of Jesus makes him difficult to approach. If that is the case, I will attempt to modify my image to accommodate the Jesus who seeks me out and who loves me, who is meek and humble of heart.

Love (III)

LOVE bade me welcome; yet my soul drew back,
                Guilty of dust and sin.
But quick-eyed Love, observing me grow slack
                From my first entrance in,
Drew nearer to me, sweetly questioning,
                If I lacked anything.

"A guest," I answered, "worthy to be here."
                Love said, "You shall be he."
"I, the unkind, ungrateful? Ah, my dear,
                I cannot look on thee."
Love took my hand, and smiling did reply,
                "Who made thy eyes but I?"

"Truth, Lord, but I have marred them; let my shame
                Go where it doth deserve."
"And know you not," says Love, "who bore the
blame?"
                "My dear, then I will serve."
"You must sit down," says Love, "and taste my meat."
                So I did sit and eat.

GEORGE HERBERT

With this week's contemplations on the public ministry of Jesus, we complete the Exercises of Phase Two. We have come to realize that the Kingdom of Jesus can be established by those generous followers who offer themselves unreservedly to Christ the King. It was the well-founded belief of Ignatius that contemplations of Jesus carrying out his Father's mission to bring forgiveness and salvation to a sinful world would inspire faith and love—love strong enough to face the cross that always cast its shadow over the landscape of the terrain that Jesus trod. Only love built on faith will be strong enough to accept—yes, even to embrace—the cross as the price to pay for bringing his message and salvation to those to whom we, his disciples, are sent. With the completion of this week's Exercises we arrive at the threshold of the Upper Chamber where Jesus ate his Last Supper with his disciples.

My Attitude: In this spirit of great generosity, the *Constitutions* of the Society of Jesus propose an approach to life modeled on an imitation of Jesus' life:

> It is likewise highly important [to remember] to how great a degree it helps and profits one in the spiritual life to abhor in its totality and not in part whatever the world loves and embraces, and to accept and desire with all possible energy whatever Christ our Lord has loved and embraced. Just as the men of the world who follow the world love and seek with such great diligence honors, fame, and esteem for a great name on earth, as the world teaches them, so those who are progressing in the spiritual life and truly following Christ our Lord love and intensely desire everything opposite. That is to say, they desire to clothe themselves with the same clothing and uniform of their Lord because of the love and reverence which He deserves, to such an extent that where there would be no offense to His Divine Majesty and no imputation of sin to the neighbor, they would wish to suffer injuries, false accusations, and affronts, and to be held and esteemed as fools (but without their giving any occasion for this), because of their desire to resemble and imitate in some manner our Creator and Lord Jesus Christ, by putting on His clothing and uniform, since it was for our spiritual profit that He clothed himself as He did. For He gave us an example that in all things possible to us we might seek, through the aid of His grace, to imitate and follow Him, since He is the way which leads men [and today Ignatius would say, "and women"] to life. (*Constitutions*, 101).

What I want and seek: I beg the Lord to choose me for the gift of the third kind of humility in order that I may find my own life more patterned according to Jesus, my God and Lord—always, of course, if this is to be for the greater praise and service of God.

Day 1 of Week 16: The Third Kind of Humility
To live as close to the truth as possible.

The third kind of humility, the ultimate kind of generosity, consists of the closest possible following of Christ in every way and is described graphically in the *Exercises* [167]. If after some time for consideration I as a retreatant want to move more in the direction of this third kind of humility, it will help much to make use of the fourfold COLLOQUY [147M]. I should beg our Lord to choose me for the gift of this third kind of humility in order that I may find my own life more patterned according to Jesus, my God and Lord—always, of course, if this is to be for the greater praise and service of God [168].

Day 2 of Week 16: John 1–11
"Let her keep this for the day of my burial!"

This anointing of the feet of Jesus by Mary, the sister of Lazarus and Martha, initiates the final episode in the "Book of Signs" whose message is that Jesus not only overcomes death, as in the story of Lazarus, but that he will confer life precisely by his death (Jn 2: 1-12: 50, CBC, Flanagan, pp. 983–1003).

It was clear to Jesus, as well as to friend and foe alike, that his life was in imminent danger. The story of the anointing closely resembles that in Mark 14: 3-9 and Matthew 26: 6-13. Both place the meal at the home of Simon the leper. The anointing was clearly a preparation for the expected imminent death of Jesus. This passage vividly draws the lines between Jesus and his followers and the chief priests and others who wanted to see both Jesus and Lazarus put to death. The considerations of the Two Standards and the Two Leaders in the early parts of the *Exercises* are now vividly concretized in this confrontational situation in which the Son of God is facing the threat of death as a criminal.

Undaunted by the cynical comments which her action aroused, Mary of Bethany, with reverence and gratitude to Jesus for restoring her brother to life, publicly anoints his feet with costly perfume and wipes them with her hair. Present in the house at Bethany, I reflect on my own reaction, my own measure of love for Jesus and my readiness to make myself a fool for His sake, if that should be required for his glory. I pray the fourfold COLLOQUY suggested in the *Exercises* [168M].

Day 3 of Week 16: Repetition
Again, I watch the anointing of Jesus and talk and think about it.

I return once more to contemplate the anointing scene, not only to observe with greater understanding what is taking place, but also to become a participant in the discussion, at least to the extent of conversing with several of the other participants (Jn 12: 1-10). Using each of my senses, I make the scene more immediate. For example, I smell and taste the foods cooked and served by Martha. Then I watch carefully as Mary pours a whole pound of very costly ointment on the feet of Our Savior. (John mentioned that the whole house was filled with its scent.) And, of course, I try to take in the varied emotions of each of the members of the scene, contrasting the attitude of Mary, for instance, with that of Judas. I will focus on the challenge to myself as I survey this scene by means of the meditation of Day 1 concerning the third kind of humility.

I will speak prayerfully to Martha, to Mary, to Lazarus, and to Jesus and ask them each to enlighten me as they face the spectre of death. I will express to each how I feel about them and ask them what response I can give in this situation. What have I done for Jesus to date? What do I want to do for him? What will I do for him and for those he loves?

Day 4 of Week 16: John 9: 1–41
The Cure of the Blind Man. "I do believe, Lord!"

This dramatic story of the cure of the man born blind portrays the struggle that he works through to remain loyal to Jesus, his benefactor, in spite of great pressures to the contrary from the establishment. Meanwhile keep in mind the Two Leaders, the Two Strategies, and the Three Classes of Persons, leading to the Election [135]. In the process he progresses from stage to stage in his belief until finally, when Jesus asks him "Do you believe in the Son of Man?. . .He said simply, 'I do believe, Lord,' and he fell on his knees in worship before him" (Jn 9: 35-38). The story is played out in seven scenes, each with layers of meaning and rich in motivation for choosing sides with Jesus.

Engage in the quadruple COLLOQUY as noted in Day 1 of this week.

Day 5 of Week 16: Repetition
"I came . . . so that those who do not see might see."

I will return to John 9: 1-41 for an APPLICATION OF THE SENSES with a focus on an assessment of my own growth in faith in Jesus as evidenced by my Election.

Day 6 of Week 16: John 12: 12–36
Last day of Jesus' public ministry: Jesus' final entry into Jerusalem

This contemplation will be concerned with what John describes as having made up the final day of Jesus' ministry to the city to which his mission is consistently directed. The appearance of a delegation of God-fearing Gentiles at this crucial moment and Jesus' response to the news of their arrival, is one of the most dramatic and most significant of the Gospel: "The hour has come for the Son of Man to be glorified" (Jn 12: 23). This contrasts with his repeated earlier protests that his "hour had not yet come" (Jn 7: 30; 8: 20). "The hour" symbolizes all those saving actions that result in salvation for all believers: the sufferings, death, and resurrection of Jesus, and his return home to the Father, all culminating in the sending of the Spirit of truth, the Paraclete.

Stanley offers a corrective translation of John's previously enigmatic verse (in chapter 12): "Father save me from this hour!" (p. 181, v.27; p. 184, v.28). The phrase has as its counterpart in John's apocalyptic writings: "Because you have kept my message of endurance, I will keep you *safe in the time of trial*" (Rv 3: 10). Thus Jesus is asking his Father to bring salvation to him "out of this hour," since in God's design it is to be the source of eternal life for all believers.

COLLOQUY: I will address a personalized COLLOQUY to each of the persons of the Holy Trinity and to our Lady, asking each to obtain for me the grace to be received under Jesus' standard: first in the highest spiritual poverty, and should the Divine Majesty be pleased thereby, and deign to choose and accept me, even in actual poverty; secondly, in bearing insults and wrongs, thereby to imitate Him better, provided only I can suffer these without sin on the part of another, and without offense of the Divine Majesty.

Day 7 of Week 16: Repetition
"The hour has come for the Son of Man to be glorified."

Repeat your contemplation of Jesus entry into Jerusalem with a slow, careful APPLICATION OF THE SENSES and a personalized COLLOQUY for each, as for Day 6 above (John 12: 12-36).

The Call

Come, my Way, my Truth, my Life:
Such a Way, as gives us breath:
Such a Truth, as ends all strife:
Such a Life, as killeth death.

Come, my Light, my Feast, my Strength:
Such a Light, as shows a feast:
Such a Feast, as mends in length:
Such a Strength, as makes his guest.

Come, my Joy, my Love, my Heart:
Such a Joy, as none can move:
Such a Love, as none can part:
Such a Heart, as joys in Love.

GEORGE HERBERT

PREPARATION FOR PHASE THREE PRAYER

St. Thomas More once prayed: "Good Lord, give us Thy grace not to read or hear this gospel of Thy bitter Passion with our eyes and ears in the manner of a pastime, but that it may with compassion so sink into our hearts that it may stretch to the everlasting profit of our souls." The purpose of the contemplations in Phase Two was to bring the "exercitant to a love of 'enlightened self-interest' for the Jesus of the public life, whereas now" in Phase Three, "he or she is being led to the love 'of friendship,' that is, no longer to love Jesus as good for me, but for his own sake. As William A. Peters remarks, 'The central point' of Phase Three 'is the great mystery of the close union between the suffering Christ and the exercitant'. . .The concentration upon the suffering Jesus and upon one's compassion here and now with him is vital to the retreatant's involvement in the Passion" [206] (Stanley, p. 203).

We must take note of the fact that in addition to the three guidelines of Phase Two (seeing the persons, hearing what they are saying, and observing what they are doing), three additional ones are now introduced by Ignatius to help achieve the purposes of Phase Three.

In addition, during this Third Phase, I should make even greater effort to labor with Christ through all his anguish, his struggle, his suffering, or what he desires to suffer [195]. At the time of the Passion, I should pay special attention to how the divinity hides itself so that Jesus seems utterly human and helpless [196]. To realize that Christ loves me so much, that he willingly suffers everything for my rejections and sins, makes me ask: "What can I, in response, do for him?" [197]. Ignatius uses the term "consider" in each of these new points thus directing the involvement of the retreatant away from self in order to focus on compassionate communion with Jesus suffering before his or her very eyes [206].

In this Phase Three of the *Exercises* we would enter heart and soul into the mystery of the Lord's passion and death. The first followers of Jesus recalled these events in great detail and set them down hour by hour. We do likewise, watching and praying with Him in His agony, conscious too that His passion is reenacted daily in the body of His poor and suffering people.

Ignatius adopts a very different strategy in Phase Three. In Phase Two from about the fifth to the twelfth week [158-61], Ignatius proposed a single mystery for contemplation [127], chosen from a range of materials with no special connection with one another except for a loose chronological arrangement. However, in Phase Three, as in the progress of Phase Two, continuity between the mysteries contemplated is recommended "to bring to mind frequently the life and mysteries of Christ our Lord, beginning with his Incarnation up to the point or mystery which I am going to contemplate" [130]. In Phase Three there is an evident concern to link the several mysteries of the Passion to each other [190-91 and 201], and to trace Jesus' movements from one place to another [208].

During the final days of Phase Three, the unity of the whole Passion story is to be contemplated. "In place of exercises that Ignatius refers to as Repetitions and Application of the Senses 'one is to consider. . .as frequently as possible how the sacred body of Christ our Lord remained separated apart from his soul, and one will call to mind where and how it was buried. And in the same way one is to consider the loneliness of our Lady, afflicted with such great sorrow and fatigue—then in addition consider the loneliness of the disciples'" (Stanley, pp. 258-59). Ignatius appears to be of the opinion that for the retreatant to achieve the unitive prayer of the Third and Fourth Phases it is necessary to achieve a deep sense of the unity of the Passion [209].

Not uncommonly the retreatant may experience extreme dryness in or distaste for prayer in the Third Phase of the retreat, thus rendering all the more difficult the fulfillment of one's efforts "to labor with Christ" [195]. This should not be a surprise since the prayer of Jesus was apparently also very difficult. Sister Marian Cowan, C.S.J. observes that "It is much more difficult to be with someone in true compassion when we are aware of being the cause of the suffering." And her coauthor, John C. Futrell, S.J., notes that "The compassion prayed for is that coming from passionate personal love of the suffering Jesus. It is not comprehension, which is so far beyond us. . . .Remaining near this suffering will break something in our hearts." (Cowan and Futrell, pp. 119-20).

Your experience in previous phases of the retreat will prepare you without additional reminders to carry out the PREPARATION as always [190]; the GRACE or Gift that I seek [193]; and the COLLOQUY, that flows out of the meditation experience, depending on the subject matter presented in the SETTING or the Scene; and Ignatius reminds us to finish with some *specific prayer* so that the formal prayer period will have closure [198].

The Colloquy: Intensified and Enlarged

Because of the intimacy involved during the contemplations of the Passion, it might be well to review some aspects of the activity called "Colloquy." Just as in human situations of taking care of the sick or ministering to the dying, our presence is often more important than our faltering words or awkward actions, thus "to be with" Christ in His Passion describes our prayer response at this time better than any words or actions. Previously I described the colloquy as the intimate conversation between friends. Now let me enlarge that description to include the depth of feeling, love, and compassion, which allows us just *to be there*.

Sometimes, still, we may want to pour out our temptations, our fears, our hardness of heart to Christ our Lord. In times of great need, we may find the intensity of our begging reflected in our use of the fourfold colloquy. We should remember that faced with the suffering of the Passion we may have to pray even for the gift of letting ourselves want to experience it with Christ.

We may find it helpful at this time of the retreat when we discover some attachment opposed to actual poverty or a repugnance to it, or when we are not indifferent to poverty and riches, to come to Jesus our Lord in prayer and beg him to choose us to serve him in actual poverty. We should beg with a certain insistence, and we should plead for it—but always wanting what God wants for us [157].

The Contemplations of Phase Three

Ignatius provides guidance for carrying out the contemplations of Phase Three in the guidelines in the text of his *Exercises*. In comparing that original text with what follows you may note that I have modified Fleming's phraseology in such a way as to bring these guidelines for the thirty-day retreat into harmony with the Nineteenth Annotation Retreat format:

1. During Phase Three, two or three Scripture passages will usually be given for each week so that the usual repetitions are made, leading to the Application of the Senses as the final period of prayer [204M].

2. Depending upon the age, the health, and the condition of the retreatant, five to seven exercises a week are encouraged, but fewer may be more desirable because of particular circumstances [205M].

3. In Phase Three, some modifications must again be made in the helps for prayer.

Because of the subject matter of the Passion, I make an effort while rising and dressing to be sad and solemn because of the great sorrow and suffering of Christ our Lord.

Throughout the day, I am careful not to bring up pleasant thoughts, even though they are good and holy, as for example thoughts about the Resurrection and life of glory. Rather I try to maintain a certain attitude of sorrow and anguish by calling to mind frequently the labors, fatigue, and suffering which Christ our Lord endured from the time of his birth down to the particular mystery of the Passion which I am presently contemplating [206].

In a similar way, the Particular Examen of Consciousness should be applied to the exercises and my observation of the helps applicable to this phase, as was done in the previous two phases [207M].

NOTE: If we want to spend more time on the Passion, the mysteries can be so divided that, for example, only the Supper is considered in one prayer period, then Christ's washing of the feet of his Apostles in another, next the institution of the Eucharist, and finally the farewell discourse of Christ. The other mysteries which make up the total Passion account could be similarly divided up.

After the Passion has been contemplated in its various mysteries over some days, there is the possibility of devoting nearly one week to the first half of the Passion, and a second equivalent period of time to the other half, and a final period of the same length reviewing the whole of the Passion.

But if we wish to spend less time on the Passion, we could use a different mystery for each of the prayer periods, eliminating all Repetitions and Applications of the Senses. After we have finished contemplating the Passion in this way, we could spend about five to seven days just letting the Passion in its whole sweep pervade the period. In all these suggested approaches, the good progress of the retreat is always the guiding consideration [209M].

PHASE THREE OF THE EXERCISES: *Weeks 17 to 19*

Week 17: Jesus is Betrayed

Background and my attitude: There is. . .[a] remarkable renewal taking place today in the giving and the making of the Spiritual Exercises, whose vivifying influence extends beyond the limits of the formal retreat into the daily life of prayer.

Not only that, fidelity to the Exercises energizes our apostolic action. It enlarges our inner freedom to respond readily to the demands which the service of the faith may make of us. It deepens in us the self-abnegation that unites us to Christ crucified, and thus to the poverty, humiliations and sufferings by which He saved the world. (*Documents of the 32nd General Congregation of the Society of Jesus*: 208-209; Appendix 17-1).

Christ our Lord continues to labor in our world to save all men and women. I ask the Father to place me with Christ suffering in the world today.

The Grace or What I seek: I ask the Father for this gift: to be able to feel sorrow with Christ in sorrow, to be anguished with Christ's anguish, and even to experience tears and deep grief because of sufferings which Christ endures for me [193].

Day 1 of Week 17: John 13: 1–30; Matthew 26: 20–30; Mark 14: 10–26
Place me with Christ for his Last Supper.

FOCUS: Jesus serves in giving himself totally [289]. PREPARATION: I take time to make the usual preparatory reverence and to petition that God direct everything in my day more and more to his praise and service [190].

SETTING: To enter as fully as I can into the preparations for the Passover Meal and into the whole event we call the Last Supper is my purpose in this contemplation. It goes beyond picturing the scene or reading the account in words. I try to listen to the way words are spoken. I attempt to see the expression on the face, I am present with as heightened an awareness as I can muster, so that I enter into the mystery I am contemplating. The Gospel accounts depict the preparations, the Supper itself, Christ's washing of the feet of his Apostles, his giving of his Body and Blood in the Eucharist, and his final words to them [191, 192, 194–97].

As Jesus gives me Eucharist I remember that I am Eucharist, that God takes me, gives thanks over me, breaks me, and gives me as gift to His people to be his presence among them. Jesus interrupts the farewell meal with his disciples at Passover to show by his example that service, even to the washing of one another's feet, is not only the role of one who would be his disciple, but is the prophetic action that explains the meaning of his death.

Read meditatively phrase by phrase or sentence by sentence the text or texts cited above. Do this according to Ignatius' Second Method of Praying. Keep in mind Ignatius' three points carried over from Phase Two [195–97], and especially consider the three additional points specific to Phase Three by referring to my commentary in the Preparation for Phase Three Prayer (see pages 120-23).

COLLOQUY: I speak to Jesus, my Lord and Savior, and stay with him through everything that happens. I close the period with an Our Father [198].

Day 2 of Week 17: John 13: 1–30
Jesus and his guests at his leave-taking meal.

This passage consists of three parts: 1) a solemn pre-Passover statement about his "hour" and his faithful love for his own; 2) the prophetic symbolism of the washing of feet; and 3) the account of how the beloved disciple achieves his identity.

JESUS DECLARES HIMSELF BEFORE THE PASSOVER
1. Several of Jesus' most symbolic actions have already taken place near the Passover, such as the cleansing of the Temple (Jn 2: 13), a prophetic proclamation of a new order of worship of the "Father in Spirit and truth" (Jn 4: 21-24), and the feeding of the crowd near the Sea of Galilee (Jn 6: 1-14), an event "depicted as having messianic and Eucharistic significance." Verse 1 is the first explicit mention of Jesus' love for his disciples. "John has intentionally reserved for the second part of his Gospel the treatment of the theme of love, particularly Christian love" (Stanley, p. 194). The earlier chapters, on the other hand, are mainly devoted to clarifying the point that genuine faith must be firmly based on the word of Jesus.

JESUS EXPLAINS THE WASHING OF THE FEET
2. John's description of the washing of the feet may be divided into two parts: what Jesus did and said (Jn 13: 2-11), and how in a commentary Jesus interpreted the symbolism of his servile act (Jn 13: 12-20).

In that second part, Jesus elaborates the meaning of the foot-washing. Even so, Jesus concludes that "What I am doing, you do not understand now, but you will understand later" (verse 7).

John had already indicated (Jn 2: 22; 12: 16) that "His disciples did not understand this at first, but when Jesus had been glorified they remembered that these things were written about him." Through Jesus' sending of the Advocate [the Paraclete] they were gifted with "remembering" (Jn 14: 26).

After completing the foot-washing as the Servant of God, Jesus having "put his garments back on and reclined at table again," becomes once again their "Teacher" and "Lord." Jesus proclaims, "I have given you a model to follow, so that as I have done for you, you should also do." His new command, to "love one another as I love you," provides the ultimate model since Jesus is to lay down his life for his friends (see Jn 15: 12-13).

JESUS SHOWS SPECIAL AFFECTION FOR JOHN

3. Although the betrayal of Jesus by Judas is the most dramatic feature in this passage, the preoccupation of the evangelist is in introducing the unnamed disciple, "whom Jesus loved." That disciple occupies the place at table next to Jesus, and is in stark contrast to Judas. It appears that he became the beloved disciple by more fully appreciating the meaning of Jesus' mission than the others, by his being "as intimate with Jesus as Jesus is with the Father" (Brown as cited by Stanley, p. 206).

Stanley perceptively notes with regard to the phrase, "And it was night," that John's innovative reinterpretation of the evangelical tradition depicts the Passion as the "glory" of Jesus (p. 207). This insight will be highlighted especially in his presentation of the scene on Calvary, from which he has carefully removed any of the tragic or ominous details prominent in the Synoptic narratives. "Schnackenburg observes, 'for Judas, night represents the sphere of darkness into which he has fallen and, what is more, of which he has become a definitive part. . . .For Jesus, it is the hour that marks the end of his work among men (cf. 9:4). . . for the evangelist (this brief statement) only serves as a dark foil to set off the words about Jesus' glorification that follows.'"

As I contemplate Jesus and the disciples at this leave-taking meal, I come to appreciate the layers of meaning for my service of Jesus and his people as well as salvation, that this passage carries. How can I respond more fully to Jesus' invitation to become a beloved disciple? I will speak to Jesus, as a disciple whom Jesus does in fact love, and discuss my reaction to this momentous scene of salvation history of which I am an active part.

Day 3 of Week 17: Application of the Senses
Place yourself at table with Jesus and the others.

Become a participant in the leave-taking meal. Observe the persons and actions of these disciples who have been chosen for Jesus' mission. On what basis are they the best qualified for their mission? Let your eyes search the person of each of his disciples to discern, if possible, what Jesus saw in them that prompted an invitation to discipleship. What personal qualities gleaned from Scripture can you recognize as you scan their faces and hear their conversation? Do any have unattractive mannerisms that remind you of other modern disciples? Now reflect on whether Jesus' insight into their qualifications for discipleship helps you to "think as God thinks" in your relationships today. Reflect on the scene following the points suggested by Ignatius for Phase Three.

Day 4 of Week 17: Matthew 26: 30–46; Mark 14: 32–44
The Agony and the betrayal in the Garden

FOCUS: Jesus seeks only the will of his Father [290].
SETTING: The Gospels give the details of the event: Christ and his disciples leave the Upper Room to go towards the garden of Gethsemane. There Jesus takes Peter, James, and John, and goes apart to pray. He experiences such turmoil of spirit that, as Mark portrays it, his sweat becomes as drops of blood. Waking his sleepy disciples, he faces the mob, is identified by the kiss of Judas, and is led away to the house of Annas. I labor to enter as fully into the account as I possibly can [201, 202].

Read meditatively, phrase by phrase or sentence by sentence, the text or texts cited above according to Ignatius' Second Method of Praying as indicated earlier in the Preparation for this third phase prayer.

Day 5 of Week 17: Matthew 26: 30–46; Mark 14: 27–44; Luke 22: 39–46
Repetition of the contemplation of Jesus' agony in the Garden.

Matthew begins this narrative by saying, "Then, after singing a hymn, they went out to the Mount of Olives." The hymn "collection" referred to is the Hallel (Pss 113-18). It includes hymns of praise of the greatness and goodness of the True God and thanksgiving to the Savior of Israel. After arriving at Gethsemane, or the "olive-press" which is a small olive garden on the Mount of Olives and a short distance from the east gate of Jerusalem, Jesus makes three predictions recounted by Mark in chapter 14: 1) "All of you will have your faith shaken" because the sheep, his followers, will be dispersed when the shepherd is struck down (v. 27); **2)** "after I have been raised up, I shall go before you to Galilee" (v. 28); and **3)** Peter will deny him three times "before the cock crows twice" (v. 30), much to the distress of the loyal-to-death, but weary Peter.

Jesus told the disciples to sit while he would "go over there and pray" (Mt 26: 36). "He took along Peter, James and John, and began to feel sorrow and distress." Here we witness, perhaps to our amazement, Jesus' humanity as he expresses his fear of death, "'My soul is sorrowful even to death. Remain here and keep watch with me.' He advanced a little and fell prostrate in prayer" (Mt 26: 37-39). This prayer in Gethsemane, and that reporting the Lord's Prayer (Mt 6: 5-15), are the great prayer passages of Matthew's Gospel. The effect of Jesus' prayer is that he can now face those who seek his life. If we are fearful at the prospect of death--and who is not?—we can confide our concern to Jesus who knows what that kind of distress is like.

The narratives concerning Jesus' prayer in both Matthew and Mark portray "his final acceptance of his Father's will as the ultimate act of his loving humanity; i.e., his choice to give up his life for the Father and for all people" (Mt 26: 39, 42, 45-46)(CBC, Van Linden, p. 932). The disciples are also depicted as needing motivation and strength during the critical time that Jesus is struggling in prayer (Mk 14: 40-41, 43, 45-46).

Day 6 of Week 17: Repetition
"Remain here and keep watch with me."

It is sometimes easy to fall into the attitude that prayer for Jesus was some sort of a pious pastime but unnecessary since he is God. However, Luke's Gospel emphasizes the importance of prayer in every phase of Jesus' life: "Jesus' ministry begins with prayer and ends with prayer (22: 46). . .Jesus prays in connection with healings (5: 16) and before selecting the twelve apostles (6: 12), before his prediction of his passion (9: 18), before his transfiguration (9: 28-29), and before he teaches his disciples how to pray (11: 1-2). He prays for Peter (22: 32). He prays to his Father. . .twice from the cross (23: 34,46). As Jesus had earlier made clear, the Holy Spirit will be given in response to prayer (Lk 11: 13). But Jesus at prayer is not only the model for Christians, but also the mediator of salvation. The figure of Jesus at prayer is a symbol that Jesus' power to effect salvation stems from God" (NJBC, Karris, p. 687). If we are to be mediators of salvation, how much more do we need to pray than did Jesus, who was so diligent in praying.

"As with the temptation (Mt 4: 1-11), the whole scene, as well as the whole passion, can be read as a commentary on the command to love God with all one's heart, soul, and strength, in which Jesus loves his heavenly Father perfectly with his will (26: 39), his soul (v. 38), and his external well-being" (v. 45) (NJBC, Viviano, p. 670).

Day 7 of Week 17: Application of the Senses
Observe and participate in the agony; pray and keep watch.

Become an observer and even a participant in the agony, prayer, and keep watch. Observe the persons and actions, especially of the three disciples chosen by Jesus to watch with him. Reflect on the scene following the points suggested by Ignatius earlier. Speak to Jesus and pray to come to a heightened insight as to the importance of prayer in your life!

When we enjoy consolation, prayer is easy and we feel close to God. When we experience desolation and emotional distress, prayer may become very difficult and the temptation to abandon prayer and turn to diversions may be very strong. This may be especially true when we are going through our own passion and death, unless we can link our distress to that of Jesus.

The attitude of one who has reached out for the third degree of humility is that of accepting and even desiring suffering, humiliations, and setbacks out of a desire to share in the passion and death of Jesus. How such an outlook would give solace to those suffering injustices, homelessness, unwarranted accusations and the like! Is this not the attitude that Jesus wished to foster in his disciples by saying "unless a grain of wheat falls to the ground and dies, it remains just a grain of wheat; but if it dies, it produces much fruit" (Jn 12: 24).

"From a Norman Crucifix of 1632"

I am the great sun, but you do not see me
I am your husband, but you turn away
I am the captive, but you do not free me
I am the captain you will not obey

I am the truth, but you will not believe me
I am the city, where you will not stay
I am your wife, your child, but you will leave me
I am the God to whom you will not pray

I am your counsel, but you do not hear me
I am the lover whom you will betray
I am the victor, but you do not cheer me
I am the holy dove whom you will slay

I am your life, but if you will not name me
Seal up your soul with tears and never blame me.

CHARLES CAUSLEY

Week 18: *Jesus Suffers Injustice, Insults, and Torture*

My Attitude: We may adapt a statement of the 32nd General Congregation of the Society of Jesus to the spirit that underlies this stage of the Exercises:

> "Availability for the meanest tasks, or at least the desire to be thus available, is part of the identity" of any man or woman who would be a companion of Jesus. "When he offers to distinguish himself in the service of the Eternal King, when he asks to be received under His standard, when he glories with Ignatius in being placed by the Father 'with the Son,' he does so not in any spirit of prideful privilege, but in the spirit of Him who 'emptied himself to assume the condition of a slave, even to accepting death, death on a cross.'" Christ our Lord continues to labor in our world to save all men and women. He continues to be tortured in His body (No. 40).

What I want and seek: I ask the Father for this gift: to be able to feel sorrow with Christ in sorrow, to be anguished with Christ's anguish, and even to experience tears and deep grief because of the afflictions which Christ endures for me and for the world.

Day 1 of Week 18: Mark 14: 44–54 and 66–68
Go with Jesus from the Garden of Olives to the house of Annas.

FOCUS: Jesus lives his passion [291]. From the considerations of Christ our King [91-99], and the Nativity [110-17], it is clear that Ignatius had in mind that they should be a preparation for this—the Passion. The cross casts its shadow from the hill of Calvary over the whole landscape upon which Jesus' and our own adventuresome lives are played out.

Most modern biblical scholars agree that the earliest Passion narratives began with the arrest of Jesus. Matthew and Luke, following Mark, have inserted introductory stories, the most important being that of the Last Supper (Mk 14: 12-26). It contains a liturgical account of the institution of the Eucharist (vv. 22-24). John, however, omits the agony in the garden since he had incorporated elements of it in his story of Jesus and the Greeks (Jn 12: 20-33; see Day 6 in Week 16 of Phase Two).

Throughout this scene Jesus is portrayed as the "Shepherd" (Mk 14: 27) who twice interrupts his prayer (vv. 37, 40) to look after the well being of his "sheep," and who issues an order to his captors, "So if you are looking for me, let these men go" (Jn 18: 8).

Other Gospel accounts of this part of the passion are presented in Matthew 26: 47-58; Luke 22: 47-65; and John 18: 1-27.

Day 2 of Week 18: Matthew 26: 57-75; Mark 14: 53-72
However reluctantly, walk in Peter's shoes from the house of Annas to the house of Caiaphas.

FOCUS: Jesus lives his passion. Matthew and Mark trace the treachery of plotting Jesus' death to the chief priests and the entire Sanhedrin [292] who "kept trying to obtain false testimony against Jesus in order to put him to death, but they found none, though many false witnesses came forward" (Mt 26: 59-60; Mk 14: 55-59).

Throughout history, how many have shared Jesus' fate in being victims of false testimony? Many have paid for the treachery and malicious conduct of others with their lives, and all have been united in solidarity with Jesus in the disgrace and distress caused by such debased conduct.

Meanwhile, Peter kept following Jesus at a distance—plagued by the ambivalence of his desire to maintain solidarity with Jesus and of his great fear of similar mistreatment. As a result and culminating in a shock, Peter denied Jesus three times as his Master had predicted he would. All at once, as Mark records in chapter 14, he recognized that Jesus' prediction of his unfaithfulness had been fulfilled (v. 30), and so Peter wept bitter tears of remorse and disappointment (v. 72). Other Gospel passages containing an account of this part of the Passion are in Luke 22: 31-34 and John 18: 24-27.

Day 3 of Week 18: Mark 15
Again, follow Jesus—this time from the house of Caiaphas to the house of Pilate.

FOCUS: Jesus lives his passion. Read slowly and prayerfully Mark 15 and/or one or more of the Gospel passages that treat the same part of Jesus' passion [293], namely Matthew 27: 1-26; Luke 23: 1-25; John 18: 28–39; 19: 1–16. As you do so, become aware of the rich and varied meanings that the Word of God has for you in helping you deal with the specific and concrete situations in your life.

Day 4 of Week 18: Luke 23: 6–11
Follow again, from the house of Pilate to the house of Herod, in spite of your shame and fright.

FOCUS: Jesus lives his passion. The appearance of Jesus before Herod is recounted only in Luke's Gospel [294]. Herod had been an important figure in Luke since he became curious about Jesus (Lk 9: 7-9; 13: 31-33). Jesus' silence in his presence, however, indicates that Jesus rewards faith, not curiosity, as is pointed out repeatedly elsewhere (Lk 7: 50; 8: 48, 50; 17: 19).

Day 5 of Week 18: Matthew 27: 1–26
Follow and watch as the "system" sends Jesus from Herod back to Pilate.

FOCUS: Jesus lives his passion. Pilate, finding no guilt in Jesus, and yet correctly recognizing that the crowd would settle for nothing less than Jesus' death, finally compromised away Jesus' very life [295]. Pilate declares Jesus innocent and places the responsibility for his death on the crowd who willingly accept that awesome responsibility (Mt 27: 24-26). Other accounts of the same part of Jesus' passion may be found in Luke: 23: 20–25; Mark 15: 12–15; and John 18: 28–31; 19: 15–16.

Day 6 of Week 18: Repetition
Where is Jesus suffering and unjustly imprisoned today?

Return to the scenes of this week's meditations and especially to those that have the greatest meaning for you in your current stage of spiritual growth. Pray that you may be freed from the pervasive compromising and treacherous spirit that brought about Jesus' death at the hands of those who knew him innocent but lacked the courage to face great opposition.

Where in our world today is Jesus suffering or bearing insults? Where is Jesus unjustly imprisoned today? Jesus told us the answer long ago in a parable: "When did I see you hungry, and I fed you? When did I see you in prison and I visited you? When did I see you naked, and clothed you, Lord?" Jesus' response is most enlightening, because he says that he is everywhere. "As long as you did it to one of my unfortunate brothers and sisters you did it to me." To each of them therefore, you can give the name, Jesus. They are in our day the anointed ones, carrying out Jesus' work as savior.

Day 7 of Week 18: Application of the Senses
Place yourself among those in the crowd who were "trying to obtain false testimony against Jesus."

Become a spectator and even an active participant in the richly rewarding and yet horrifying scenes in these Scriptural passages that recount Jesus' humiliation and unjust trial because he proclaimed himself the Messiah and Son of God. Using all the senses make these scenes as vivid as possible so that their meaning for you may be as salvific as possible.

I pray with all the sincerity I can muster, so that I may desire to imitate Jesus in bearing insults, wrongs, and humiliations provided no offense is given to God.

Still Falls the Rain   *(The Raids, 1940. Night and Dawn)*

Still falls the Rain—
Dark as the world of man, black as our loss—
Blind as the nineteen hundred and forty nails
Upon the Cross.

Still falls the Rain
With a sound like the pulse of the heart that is changed to the hammerbeat
In the Potters' Field, and the sound of the impious feet
On the Tomb:
     Still falls the Rain
In the Field of Blood where the small hopes breed and the human brain
Nurtures its greed, that worm with the brow of Cain.

Still falls the Rain
At the feet of the Starved Man hung upon the Cross.
Christ that each day, each night, nails there, have mercy on us—
On Dives and on Lazarus:
Under the Rain the sore and the gold are as one.

Still falls the Rain—
Still falls the Blood from the Starved Man's wounded Side
He bears in his Heart all wounds,—those of the light that died,
The last faint spark
In the self-murdered heart, the wounds of the sad uncomprehending dark,
The wounds of the baited bear,—
The blind and weeping bear whom the keepers beat
On his helpless flesh. . .the tears of the hunted hare.

Still falls the Rain—
Then—O Ile leape up to my God: who pulles me doune—
See, see where Christ's blood streams in the firmament:
It flows from the Brow we nailed upon the tree
Deep to the dying, to the thirsting heart
That holds the fires of the world,—dark-smirched with pain
As Caesar's laurel crown.

Then sounds the voice of One who like the heart of man
Was once a child who among beasts has lain—
"Still do I love, still shed my innocent light, my Blood, for thee."

EDITH SITWELL

Week 19: The King Mounts His Throne of Glory

Ignatius' Attitude, My own Attitude: The following account is taken from Young's translation of *The Spiritual Journal of St. Ignatius Loyola* (pp. 15-17):

> Saturday [February 23, 1544]—While preparing the altar, the thought of Jesus occurred to me. I felt a movement to follow Him, it seemed to me interiorly, since He was the head of the Society. . . . .This thought moved me to devotion and to tears. . . .I went along with these thoughts and vested while they increased. . .and think-ing that the appearance of Jesus was in some way from the Most Holy Trinity, I recalled the day when the Father placed me with the Son. As I finished vesting with this intention of impressing on my mind the name of Jesus. . .a fresh attack of tears and sobbing came upon me. . . .As I held the Blessed Sacrament in my hands, the word came to me with an intense interior movement never to leave Him for all heaven and earth. . . .

> Sunday [February 24, 1544]—While preparing the altar and vesting, I saw a representation of the name of Jesus with much love, confirmation and increased desire to follow Him.
> All through the Mass very great devotion, on the whole, with many tears, and several times loss of speech, all devotion and feel-ing being directed by Jesus. . . .Having finished Mass, I had during the prayer that same feeling towards the Son. . .and felt that it was given to me through Jesus, when He showed Himself to me.
> Later, at the fire, there was a fresh representation of Jesus with great devotion and movement to tears. Later as I walked through the streets, I had a vivid representation of Jesus with interior movements and tears. After dinner. . .I felt or saw Jesus, had many interior movements and many tears. . . .
> At these times, when I sensed or saw Jesus, I felt so great a love within me that I thought that nothing could happen in the fu-ture that would separate me from Him.

Christ the Lord continues to labor in our world to save all men and women. He still follows the way of the cross toward Calvary. I ask the Father to place me with Christ crucified in the world today.

The gift I want and desire: I ask the Father for this gift: to be able to feel sorrow with Christ in sorrow, to be anguished with Christ's an-guish, and even to experience tears and deep grief because of all the afflictions which Christ endures for me.

Day 1 of Week 19: John 19: 13-22
From the house of Pilate to the Cross, inclusive.

FOCUS: Jesus lives his passion. The theme of Jesus' kingship and the cost of discipleship dominate the Passion narrative. The day and the time at which Jesus was handed over to them to be crucified were of great significance to John: "It was the day for Passover-preparation, and the time about noon" when the Jewish clergy undertook the ceremonial butchering of the paschal lambs. John had previously referred to Jesus as "the Lamb of God" (Jn 1: 29, 36), but now through his death Jesus would replace the old, and now outdated rituals.

Unlike the three Synoptics, John interprets the Passion as Jesus' "glory." With some of his other companions I watch along the way to Calvary. I am grateful for the women who tried to comfort him and for Simon, portrayed as the ideal disciple, who helped shoulder the cross according to Mt 27: 32; Mk 15: 21; and Lk 23: 26. John portrays Jesus as carrying his own cross, probably remembering the symbolism of the story in which Abraham put the wood needed for the sacrifice on the shoulders of his son, Isaac (Gn 22: 6).

Hugo Rahner (p. 132) cites an early Jesuit authority on the *Exercises* who states that the Third Phase is calculated "to find the heart of Christ in the midst of the turmoils of his Passion, and to rouse ourselves to enter into community with the crucified Christ, so that" each of us "can say. . .'my love is crucified!'" John, beginning with Chapter 13, repeatedly places emphasis upon and demonstrates Jesus' love for his followers.

COLLOQUY: In it pray to Jesus' Mother, Mary, asking her to share with you her understanding of, and her way of coming to accept, the sufferings of Jesus' Passion as his "glory."

Day 2 of Week 19: John 19: 23-37
Jesus dies on the Cross.

As we contemplate the crucifixion and death of Jesus [297] it is essential to be mindful of the entire Paschal mystery. Jesus' thumb-nail parable from planting and harvesting sums it up: "Amen, amen, I say to you, unless a grain of wheat falls to the ground and dies, it remains just a grain of wheat; but if it dies, it produces much fruit" (Jn 12: 25).

John replaces the narrative of the Synoptics (Mt 27: 35-44; Mk 15: 29-32; Lk 23: 33-37) with the pathos of Jesus nailed to the cross and dying, with his Mother and beloved disciple standing by. We should note that not only does Jesus entrust his mother to the beloved disciple, but also that the disciple is handed over to the care of Mary as his mother. Can we doubt that Jesus intended to remind his followers of the mother who gave birth to him and to the community of the people of God?

What were Jesus' thoughts and feelings, in spite of the excruciating pain of crucifixion, as he became aware that the scriptures had been perfectly fulfilled and that this first phase of his work on earth was drawing to a close?

COLLOQUY: In your fourfold colloquy, ask Mary to share with you insights into the meaning of Jesus' life and mission and your place in that great work of sanctifying every sphere of human endeavor. Speak to Jesus on the Cross, to his Father and our Father, and to the Holy Spirit waiting to be sent as our Advocate when Jesus draws his last breath and rises gloriously.

Day 3 of Week 19: John 19: 38–42
From the Cross to the Sepulchre, inclusive.

FOCUS: We enter into the sense of loss, of emptiness, of waiting [298]. I join the small procession to the tomb.

The burial of Jesus occupies a central place in the loving attention, reflection and devotion of his earliest followers. The burial was one of the four articles of faith in the earliest creed known to us (1 Cor 15: 3-11), as was the descent of our glorified Savior to those who had died (Rom 14: 9). Ignatius speaks specifically of Jesus going to the abode of the dead to take the just souls to heaven [219].

Here John introduces Nicodemus, a disciple of Jesus in secret because of his influential position as a prominent and wealthy member of the Sanhedrin (Jn 3: 1; 7: 50-52). Mark describes him as one seeking the Kingdom of God. Nicodemus, a teacher in Israel (Jn 3: 10), contributed an impressive gift of burial ointments, one that befits his standing in the community. The evangelists are unanimous in crediting Joseph of Arimathea, also a secret disciple, with arranging Pilate's permission to take Jesus' body for burial. Other passages dealing with Jesus' burial are in Matthew 27: 57-61; Mark 15: 42-47; Luke 23: 50-56.

COLLOQUY: In your prayer express what you feel as a result of contemplating this scene of death, that to many, if not all, the disciples must have seemed a tragic ending of all their dreams and hopes.

Day 4 of Week 19: Isaiah 52: 13–53: 1–12
The sinless suffering servant is triumphant.

I listen prayerfully to the fourth song of the servant of Yahweh who is one with all who sorrow, but who is separate from them by reason of the innocence of his life and total dedication to God. This last of the four "Servant of the Lord" oracles is a moving description of the sinless Servant of God, who rescues his people from their sins by his voluntary suffering, saving them from the punishment they deserve at God's hands, the perfect expression of expiatory suffering. It is only in Jesus that this prophecy is completely fulfilled.

In chapter 53 of Isaiah, the speaker is no longer Yahweh but the Deutero-Isaiah, or his disciples. And the theme is loneliness, as the servant is rejected by his own people (Is 53: 1–3). I pray, with all the sincerity I can find within me, that I may desire to imitate Jesus in bearing insults, wrongs and humiliations without any offense being given to God. How many of us perceive that we are not well understood by those whom we love most, not uncommonly a source of bitter disappointment.

Apply this Old Testament story to Jesus, Suffering servant of the New Testament, and let your heart speak to him as you pray that you may work and not get weary, suffer and bear your cross like Jesus, the Suffering Servant, who teaches us how to suffer and even how to love in our suffering.

Day 5 of Week 19: The Cross and The Crucifix
Place yourself on Calvary or on the way to it.

It may be helpful in creating an atmosphere of prayerfulness to apply the Second Method of Prayer [249-257] to John 19: 38-42 (above, as in Day 3). It may also be beneficial in helping to deepen your silence to meditate in subdued light or a darkened room with a lighted candle or vigil light. Instinctively we tend to relax and focus our thoughts and emotions to an extraordinary degree. Hold the crucifix in your hand—the crucifix of your rosary will do.

Place yourself in any one of the scenes on Calvary or along the Way of the Cross and observe the actions, reactions and emotions of others in the scene. What do you feel? Use all of your senses in turn to render the scene as vividly present as it was to those who witnessed it as it was happening.

After a few minutes, or whenever you feel impelled to do so, speak to Jesus, to Mary or to the Apostles and share your emotions, your hopes, your sadness, your gratitude because Jesus is doing this to lift the burden of sin and sinfulness from you, me and the human race. If you are in the company of those with whom you can share these moments, as for example in a prayer group or in the weekly meeting of the retreat group, hold the crucifix and pray aloud. It may be helpful after a period of silent meditation, or after praying aloud, to pass the crucifix to the next person who can share in silent prayer or aloud according to a felt need.

I accompany Mary, the Mother of Jesus, away from the tomb back to the house where she is staying. I stay with her, I wait with her, I listen to her as she shares with me all those things she has pondered in her heart. I listen to her memories of her Son. I weep with her, I hope with her. And I tell her who I am and who I want myself to be.

Day 6 of Week 19: Repetition
Consider those elements from the preceding days that are most helpful.

> *O King of the Friday*
> *Whose limbs were stretched on the cross,*
> *O Lord who did suffer*
> *The bruises, the wounds, the loss,*
> *We stretch ourselves*
> *Beneath the shield of thy might,*
> *Some fruit from the tree of thy passion*
> *Fall on us this night!*
>
> FROM THE IRISH

Day 7 of Week 19: Repetition of the whole Passion
"In those dark moments, O God, grant that I may understand."

Because it is so timely in the context of the subject matter of this week, contemplate your own diminishment and death—your apparent failures and transfiguration (Teilhard de Chardin, *The Divine Milieu*, pp. 84-90). In the light of your own response, savor and perhaps rephrase the author's Colloquy, entitled Communion through Diminishment (pp. 89-90). In this last reference Teilhard de Chardin sums up the spirit of this exercise where he prays: "In those dark moments, O God, grant that I may understand that it is you. . .who are painfully parting the fibers of my being in order to penetrate to the very marrow of my substance and bear me away within yourself."

You may also want to use the brief prayer below. It is attributed to Saint Thomas Aquinas and is said to have been written by him on the wall of a cave during a violent storm.

> *O Cross, my sure salvation,*
> *O Cross, which I ever adore,*
> *O Cross of my Savior,*
>   *be with me.*
> *O Cross, my refuge*
>   *is in thee.*

PREPARATION FOR PHASE FOUR PRAYER

"Blessed be the God and the Father of our Lord Jesus Christ, the Father of compassion and God of all encouragement, who encourages us in our every affliction so that we may be able to encourage those who are in any afliction with the encouragement with which we ourselves are encouraged by God. For as Christ's sufferings overflow to us, so through Christ does our encouragement also overflow" (2 Corinthians 1:3-5).

The consolation, the joy, the new surge of life that the Risen Christ bestows upon His followers from Easter morning until this present day is the gift we beg for now in the Fourth Phase. Hopkins captured Ignatius' thought in these words: "Let Him easter in us, be a dayspring to the dimness of us, be a crimson-cresseted east."

In all our contemplations we observe how the risen Lord manifests the true splendor of the Godhead by consoling and strengthening those whom the Father loves. And, not long before his death, a friend and fellow scientist expressed it for us thus:

Trumpets echo; we hear their cloistered call;
And hope diffuses through tormented earth.
We recall the promise of December
When angel brass declared Messiah's birth.
Good Friday's pall brought to a muted end
The Lenten days of fasting and of prayer
And Saturday a soundless empty void
Without Christ's timbre moving through the air.

Like Mary, now we hear the angel's call
And know the Gospel message for us all
That death is not our predetermined end.
Sing out! Proclaim the Easter news today!
Praise Jesus Christ on this triumphant day!
And let your voice with saints and angels blend.

DAVID R. WONES

Faith Insight into the "Why" of Christian Optimism

Ignatius offers thirteen post-resurrection appearances as possible contemplations [218–29, 299–311]. While the first three points for the retreatant remain the same as in previous phases, Ignatius, in the fourth point, advises the retreatant "to consider how the divinity, which seemed to hide itself in the Passion, now appears and shows itself so marvelously in the most holy Resurrection by its true and most holy effects" [223]. As the fifth point he counsels "to realize that the role of consoler which Christ performs in each of his resurrection appearances is the same role he performs now in my life" [224]. This is a faith insight into the reason why I can live my life with true Christian optimism.

Throughout Phase Four, take the time for the usual preparatory reverence and petition that God direct everything in your day more and more to his praise and service. According to the changed circumstances of the Setting, let your fourfold colloquy be directed to Mary, the Risen Lord, the Father and the Holy Spirit and always close with the Lord's prayer or some other appropriate prayer [225M].

In all the contemplations of Phase Four the mysteries of the Resurrection through the Ascension inclusive may be shortened or lengthened by a selection or division of the various mysteries. The freedom shown in Phase Three to engage in repetitions, application of the senses, shortening or lengthening of the mysteries on the Passion should likewise be the guide here [226]. Additionally, it is more in keeping with the atmosphere of relaxed consolation in Phase Four to have no more than four or five periods of prayer within the week, although there could be three passages of Scripture presented for contemplation. The prayer of the fourth or fifth day centers on those aspects of the preceding three contemplations which moved the retreatant with greater spiritual relish [227M].

As I allow the Scripture passage to present the setting for prayer, certain elements will provide me with a focus. I should be sure to let these focal points direct my attention during the prayer period [228].

In Phase Four I make some modifications in the helps toward making the whole day consistently prayerful. As soon as I awake, I recall the atmosphere of joy which pervades this Phase and review the particular mystery which I am about to contemplate.

Throughout this week, I try to keep myself in a mood which is marked by happiness and spiritual joy. As a result, anything in my environment—the sun and warm weather or the white cover of snow, all the different beauties of nature, and so on—is used to reinforce the atmosphere of consolation. Obviously, during this period, penance is not in keeping with the total movement, and so only the usual temperance and moderation in all things is encouraged [229M].

Easter

Rise heart; thy Lord is risen. Sing his praise
　　　　　　Without delayes,
Who takes thee by the hand, that thou likewise
　　　　　　With him mayst rise:
That, as his death calcined thee to dust,
His life may make thee gold, and much more just.

Awake, my lute, and struggle for thy part
　　　　　　With all thy art
The cross taught all wood to resound his name
　　　　　　Who bore the fame
His stretched sinews taught all strings, what key
Is best to celebrate this most high day.

Confort both heart and lute, and twist a song
　　　　　　Pleasant and long:
Or since all musick is but three parts vied
　　　　　　And multiplied:
O let thy blessed Spirit bear a part,
And make up our defects with his sweet art.

I got me flowers to straw thy way;
I got me boughs off many a tree:
But thou wast up by break of day,
And broughtst thy sweets along with thee.

The Sunne arising in the East,
Though he give light, and th' East perfume;
If they should offer to contest
With thy arising, they presume.

Can there be any day but this,
Though many sunnes to shine endeavour?
We count three hundred, but we misse;
There is but one, and that one ever.

GEORGE HERBERT

PHASE FOUR OF THE EXERCISES: *Weeks 20 to 24*

Week 20: *Christ the Lord Conquers Death*

My authentic Ignatian Attitude: If we wish to be faithful to the special character of our Christian vocation as companions of Jesus, no matter what else that vocation entails, "we must 'contemplate' our world as Ignatius did his, that we may hear anew the call of Christ dying and rising in the anguish and aspirations of men and women" (*Documents of the 32nd General Congregation of the Society of Jesus*, no. 68). The risen Lord is with us as He promised, to console us and to give us His gifts, so that we may console those who suffer in the world today.

What I want and desire: I beg for the gift of being able to enter into the joy and consolation of Jesus in the victory of his risen life [221].

Day 1 of Week 20: Contemplation of the Risen Lord
The first appearance of Christ our Lord is to his Mother, Mary.

FOCUS: The risen Jesus [218] is first seen in his role as consoling Mary his mother [299]. The SETTING for this contemplation is left to your heart and to your imagination, since there is no Scriptural basis to guide your thoughts. In the usual way, try to enter into this contemplation as fully as you can. Ignatius understood that the first person to whom Jesus would appear would be his mother. You can easily imagine the excitement of Jesus in wanting to share the joy of his resurrection with his Mother who had stood by him throughout the Passion. Let the delight and the love of this encounter permeate your being [219–20, 222–24].

Day 2 of Week 20: John 20: 1–18
"I have seen the Lord!"

FOCUS: With Mary Magdalene I hear my name, and respond with joy. Although women were not recognized by the early Christian Church as official witnesses, it seems clear that Jesus appeared first of all to women. Mary of Magdala (not to be confused with Mary of Bethany, the sister of Lazarus and Martha) had stayed near the cross with Mary, the mother of Jesus, and with the beloved disciple (Jn 19: 25–26). Luke also mentions this Mary of Magdala--traditionally identified as the sinner in the preceding passage (Lk 7: 37)—as one of the wealthy women who out of gratitude for having been delivered from evil spirits or disease had helped to provide for Jesus and his disciples (Lk 8: 1–3).

By reason of her desolate concern the Magdalene had come to the tomb while it was still dark only to discover that the body of her Master was missing. Visualize the heartwarming scene in which she mistook Jesus for a gardener, her petition to him to tell her where Jesus' body had been placed so that she could take him away herself, and her ecstatic joy at recognizing Jesus. Her deep affection and her determination to undertake the nearly impossible task of carrying Jesus' body away singlehandedly, shows her readiness to accept the gift of faith in her risen Savior which he gives her merely by calling her by her name, "Mary." She thus became the first recipient of Christian faith from the risen Lord and the first to announce to the other disciples the Easter message.

One of the recurring themes of John the Evangelist ("Where is Jesus for me?") emerges in Jesus' question, "Woman, why are you weeping?" and Mary's response, "They have taken my Lord, and I don't know where they laid him" (Jn 20: 13).

Day 3 of Week 20: Luke 24: 13-35
"Were not our hearts burning [within us] while he spoke to us on the way?"

This magnificent story is alive with Luke's themes of journey as an image of discipleship; faith portrayed as "seeing" because the risen Christ opens the eyes of the disciples to see his true place and role in God's plan; and the closely related theme of hospitality, in which disciples who entertain the stranger will have their eyes opened. The importance of hospitality in Luke indicates that God's Kingdom has come in Jesus' sharing food with others, especially outcasts. Jesus had said at the Last Supper that he would not share food with his disciples until God's Kingdom had come (22: 16, 18)(NJBC, Karris, pp. 720-21).

In a pre-eminent way Jesus serves as the consoler of those disciples who had abandoned the following of their Master (Lk 24: 21) because what had happened did not match their expectations of what should have happened. Their Risen Lord, instead of abandoning them to their own blindness to his earlier teachings, overtakes them and explains that it was "necessary for the Messiah to suffer these things and enter into his glory" (Lk 24: 26).

"Through the disciples' concern to provide hospitality to this stranger, their sadness, foolishness and slowness of heart are transformed into joy, insight, and joyful recommitment to Jesus' way" (NJBC, Karris, p. 721). Jesus, my companion on my own journey to

Emmaus, enlightens me as to how He has been part of my history and prehistory, nourishing me in so many ways. Consoled and with heart burning within me, I want to proclaim to all: "The Lord has been raised!"

Day 4 of Week 20: Repetition
Again, console yourself with the news of the Resurrection.

Return to the most nourishing parts of the contemplations of this week.

Day 5 of Week 20: Application of the Senses
Place yourself with those who saw the risen Christ.

Return to such scenes and become an active participant in these glorious mysteries:

> Most glorious Lord of lyfe, that on this day,
>> Didst make thy triumph over death and sin:
> And having harrowd hell, didst bring away
>> Captivity thence captive us to win:
>> This joyous day, deare Lord, with joy begin,
> And grant that we, for whom thou diddest dye,
>> Being with thy deare blood clene washt from sin,
> May live for ever in felicity.
> And that thy love we weighing worthily,
>> May likewise love thee for the same againe:
> And for thy sake that all lyke deare didst buy,
>> With love may one another entertayne.
>> So let us love, deare love, lyke as we ought,
>> Love is the lesson which the Lord us taught.

EDMUND SPENSER

Week 21: The King Sends Forth His Followers, and thus the Risen Lord Shares His Mission

My Attitude: "When you send forth your spirit, they are created, and you renew the face of the earth." (Psalm 104: 30).

The Father continues to pour out the Spirit of Christ on the men and women of our day. He consoles us still, and sends us on mission to console the suffering and the poor and all who long for salvation.

What I want and desire: I ask the Father for this gift: to be able to enter into the joy and the consoling mission of Jesus in His risen life.

Day 1 of Week 21: John 20: 19–23
Jesus next places himself with his desolate disciples.

FOCUS: Christ is the life-giver [304]. Even after Mary had reported the good news that she had seen the Lord, the disciples were unconvinced—"When he had risen, early on the first day of the week, he appeared first to Mary Magdalene, out of whom he had driven seven demons. She went and told his companions who were mourning and weeping. When they heard that he was alive and had been seen by her, they did not believe" (Mk 16: 9-11). The scene opens with Jesus praying that peace may come upon his disciples (Lk 24: 36), a legacy bequeathed to them at the Last Supper, but not yet realized in them (Jn. 14: 27; 16: 33).

His disciples recognized Jesus through the wounds in his hands, feet and side, and they were joyful when they saw him. And then Jesus sent them forth with his peace, giving them the mission his Father had given him. And in words that recall God breathing on the first man and giving him life (Gn 2: 7), John continues, "And when he [Jesus] had said this, he breathed on them and said to them, 'Receive the holy Spirit. Whose sins you forgive are forgiven them, and whose sins you retain are retained'" (Jn 20: 22-23).

There is an important relationship of continuity between the earthly and risen life of Jesus, which endows the Christian "remembering" with its efficacy. . . .In fact, "remembering" is imperative for Christian prayer, which consists in "keeping Jesus in mind"—as he himself enjoined through the words of Eucharistic institution. That Ignatius was aware of this unbroken continuity is clear from the *Spiritual Exercises* [116, 206]. Moreover, Ignatius insisted that, for an effective Election, discernment must take place "while continuing to contemplate Jesus' life" [135].

"Like the fourth evangelist before him, the Saint (Ignatius) is convinced of the perennial reality of the 'mysteries of the life of our

Lord.' Thus Christian contemplation is not merely an exercise of pious imagination: it is the quintessential means of relating in faith to 'the crucified Majesty of God'" (Stanley, p. 285). Practically speaking, this observation means that it is necessary to pray to our risen Savior through the mysteries of his earthly existence. Transfigured by his glorification, they are very much part of his dynamic presence to the life of the Church and to that of each Christian. Thus the words of Jesus to his doubting disciples, huddled in the upper room of the Cenacle in fear of the Jews, are addressed to each of his modern day disciples who wishes to learn to pray.

Day 2 of Week 21: John 20: 24–31
"Blessed are those who have not seen and have believed."

FOCUS: faith in the Lord Jesus is seeing and not seeing [305]. John represents our risen Lord as having a deep concern for all who have never had a first hand relationship with him. Consequently he bestows a special blessing on those who had never seen or known Jesus, but who are believers. John subtly criticizes faith that is based solely on "seeing the signs Jesus performed" (2: 23; 3: 2; 4: 48; 6: 2; 11: 47). The story of "doubting" Thomas is not reported in any other Gospel, although we have become familiar with him in several other incidents in which we are able to learn something of his personality. In several cases Thomas asks for explanations—"How can we know the way?" (14: 5)—or makes strong statements, as for example, when Jesus plans to return to raise Lazarus from the dead: "Let us also go and die with him" (11: 16).

And when confronted by Jesus because of his incredulity (20: 27), Thomas responds as one making a final commitment to the risen Jesus with that utterly penitent and faith-filled exclamation that has deeply moved millions of the faithful throughout the ages, "My Lord and my God!" (20: 28).

Tolerant of my dimness and unbelief as he was of Thomas, Jesus delights in consoling me with the gift of renewed faith. In His loving presence I utter, "My Lord and my God!"

Day 3 of Week 21: Matthew 28: 16–20
The Great Mission—"I am with you always!"

FOCUS: Jesus is the consoler [301]. This brief ending to Matthew's Gospel is dazzling in its richness, having been called a partial fulfillment of Daniel's vision of the Son of Man. "The eleven" (Mt 28: 16) is a tragic reminder of the defection of Judas. Jesus commissions those who remain, all sinners, who had been tried during his passion and death and found wanting; but who, have regrouped to be strengthened in faith by the Risen Lord. Jesus still recruits sinners whom he invites to be his companions, and sends us forth "to make disciples of all nations" with the strengthening promise, "And behold, I am with you always" (Mt 28: 20). This promise that he will be with us in every joyful and every painful moment as we carry out his work is most reassuring and consoling.

The mountain to which reference is made is the place of revelation and transfiguration (Mt 17: 1); it has theological rather than geographical significance—a meeting place between God and His people. It could be a slum, a lab, a church, a clinic, an office, a living room, a classroom. The mountain is a place to pray. Remember that Jesus felt a deep-seated need to go regularly up to the mountain to pray.

Day 4 of Week 21: Repetition
Again, place yourself in the post-Resurrection events.

Return to those scenes, events, and persons that have proven most meaningful to you during previous contemplations this week.

Day 5 of Week 21: Application of the Senses
"And behold, I am with you always."

Return to scenes in Day 4 but become a part of the scene and involved in the activity taking place. Actively converse with Jesus, his disciples and others as you feel moved to so so.

The Prayer of the Lark

I am here! O my God.
I am here, I am here!
You draw me away from earth,
and I climb to You
in a passion of shrilling,
to the dot in heaven
where, for an instant, You crucify me.
When will you keep me forever?
Must You always let me fall
back to the furrow's dip,
a poor bird of clay?
Oh, at least
let my exultant nothingness
soar to the glory of Your mercy,
in the same hope,
until death.
Amen.

CARMEN BERNOS DE GASZTOLD
(*translated by Rumer Godden*)

Week 22: "I will ask the Father and he will give you another Advocate [Paraclete]."

An idea whose realization can transform my life: The Spirit is alive, working in the Church and in each of its members.

What I want and desire: I pray, joyfully and generously, for a deeper awareness of the presence and power of the Spirit of Jesus in all the events of my life.

Day 1 of Week 22: John 14: 15–21
"But you know [the Spirit of Truth] because it remains with you, and will be in you."

FOCUS: I recall the words of Jesus about the work of the Holy Spirit. John's Gospel contains a most consoling and reassuring promise made by Jesus on the night before he died, that he will not leave us orphaned in the aftermath of his death, resurrection and ascension. Although Jesus must go to his Father he makes a covenant with us through his disciples (Jn 14: 16-17). Various translations have been given for the Greek word *parakletos* but none quite catches the flavor of the original. A paraclete is an attorney for the defense, witness for the accused, best friend, comforter in time of distress, and intercessor. What Jesus tells us is that the Holy Spirit takes the place of the risen and ascended Jesus in the midst of the disciples, ministering in all of the ways implied by the name advocate or paraclete. These names help to recall the intimate union between the Spirit and Jesus, the first paraclete.

God, our Father, becomes present to the world in all ages through advocates: Jesus, the Spirit, the apostles, the disciples, and those who give testimony to the truth of the God we cannot see. Jesus has told us that we can bank on the help of the Spirit even in the most difficult of situations: "When they hand you over, do not worry about how you are to speak or what you are to say. You will be given at that moment what you are to say. For it will not be you who speak but the Spirit of your Father speaking through you" (Mt. 10: 19-20).

From the foregoing and from many other passages I should be reassured that far from being orphaned, I have been adopted into the intimate relationship of Jesus with the Father, through the gift of the Spirit, my paraclete. Moreover, I am assured of my effectiveness when I am on a mission for Jesus, my Savior.

Day 2 of Week 22: Acts 2: 1–41
"And they were all filled with the Holy Spirit."

FOCUS: The promise of the Spirit's coming was fulfilled when the day of Pentecost arrived. The Greek word for wind (pneuma) is the same as that for spirit, and both are associated in John 3: 8. The sound of a great rush of wind would usher in an important action of God in salvation history.

These passages deal with the birth and growth of the Church in Jerusalem through the Spirit. More specifically in the Acts 2: 1-13 the main concern is with the Pentecost event. In the next passage Luke recounts the Pentecost sermon, attributed to Peter, that declares the resurrection of Jesus and its messianic significance, and concludes with a favorable response from the audience and the acceptance of baptism (Acts 2: 14-41).

Peter's speech concludes with the prophet Joel's consoling promise, "and it shall be that everyone shall be saved who calls on the name of the Lord" (Acts 2: 21). When Peter had finished his speech and the responsive audience had asked what each one must do, "Peter [said] to them, 'Repent and be baptized, every one of you, in the name of Jesus Christ for the forgiveness of your sins; and you will receive the gift of the holy Spirit'" (Acts 2: 38).

What joy, peace of mind and gratitude I should have for having been given these precious gifts of baptism and the Holy Spirit. Spend time meditating upon the activities attributed to the Father, the Son, and the Holy Spirit and spend some time in praying to each for prayerful insights into these gifts.

Day 3 of Week 22: 1 Corinthians 12: 1–11
"One and the same Spirit produces all of these [gifts], distributing them individually to each person as he wishes."

This Scriptural passage is part of Paul's concern to remedy certain misunderstandings concerning the relative value of various spiritual gifts such as wisdom, knowledge, faith, healing, prophecy, tongues and discernment. Paul attempted to correct this deficiency by pointing out that even the most spiritual of gifts is meant for building up the "body," the Church (1 Cor 12: 12-31).

The Corinthians took persuasive eloquence as evidence for one's possession of the Spirit. Paul maintains that the point of all Christian speech is the proclamation of Christ's lordship which can only be made through the Spirit and must not be divisive. He emphasizes that without faith even gifts of the Spirit can be divisive rather than building up the Body of Christ. Prophecy or persuasive pastoral speech that achieves that goal is praised, but Paul goes on in the famous passage (1 Cor 13: 1-13) to extol love as the pre-eminent gift of the Spirit for all of the community. As I meditate on the Holy Spirit, the great gift to me from the Father, I feel impelled to turn inward where I feel the Spirit to be intimately present to me, and I pray that Jesus may truly be my Lord, taking dominion over all my unruly tendencies. I will pray that I may be inspired to use my individual gifts to be an instrument of the Lord's peace as St. Francis of Assisi has so well expressed:

> *Lord, make me an instrument of Thy peace!*
> *where there is hatred let me sow love*
> *where there is injury, pardon;*
> *where there is doubt, faith*
> *where there is despair, hope*
> *where there is darkness, light*
> *where there is war, peace*
> *where there is sadness, joy.*

Day 4 of Week 22: Repetition
God is passing by.

Return to those scenes, events and persons that have been most meaningful in the previous contemplations of this week. In times past as the wind rustled through the trees, it was said that "God is passing by." That thought has its own beauty but the reality is that we have the Holy Spirit with us always from that time when Jesus left our Earth.

Day 5 of Week 22: Application of the Senses
"If I have all faith. . . but do not have love, I am nothing."

Become a part of that scene and event that is most meaningful to you and visualize it as vividly as possible. Address the Holy Spirit in your prayer, even in a non-verbal Colloquy , or without mental pictures, if you wish and in the spirit of the anonymous author of *The Cloud of Unknowing*. Even though you may at times feel that you are "blocked off" as if by a cloud when you reach up toward Jesus, try a prayer of silent repose. Saint Teresa of Avila called it the prayer of quiet. This kind of prayer consists of silent union with the Trinity, during which words may well up in your heart from time to time.

Little Gidding   IV

The dove descending breaks the air
With flame of incandescent terror
Of which the tongues declare
The one discharge from sin and error.
The only hope, or else despair
    Lies in the choice of pyre or pyre—
    To be redeemed from fire by fire.

Who then devised the torment? Love.
Love is the unfamiliar Name
Behind the hands that wove
The intolerable shirt of flame
Which human power cannot remove.
    We only live, only suspire
    Consumed by either fire or fire.

T. S. ELIOT

Week 23: *The Prodigal God: Contemplation on His Love*

An idea whose realization will transform my life: the Father, Son, and Holy Spirit are always at work sharing themselves with me. This sharing empowers me to become a contemplative-in-action, finding God in all things. It will be helpful for me "to be ever mindful of what Saint Ignatius says about love, that it consists in sharing what one has, what one is, with those one loves." (*Documents of the 32nd General Congregation of the Society of Jesus, Jesuits Today*, No. 28).

What I want and desire: I ask the Father to give me an intimate knowledge of the many gifts received, that filled with gratitude for all, I may in all things love and serve the Divine Majesty.

Love expresses itself in full, mutual sharing

Remember that love ought to show itself in deeds and not just in words; and that love expresses itself in a full, mutual sharing, such that the lover and the beloved always give and receive from one another, fully, without reserve, of everything that one has and is. For example, a lover gives and shares with the beloved personal gifts, possessions, including money, prestige, honors and position. In love, one always wants to give to the other [230-31M].

PREPARATION: It is as always in previous weeks. I may find it especially helpful to imagine myself standing before God and all his saints who are praying for me [232]. The GRACE or GIFT THAT I SEEK is the gift of an intimate knowledge of all the sharing of goods which God does in his love for me. Filled with gratitude, I want to be empowered to respond just as totally in my love and service of him [233].

Four points present the subject matter for my prayer, one for each day's prayer.

Day 1 of Week 23: Contemplation on the love of God
God's many, great gifts to me. What ought I to give in return!

I reflect on the gifts of creation, redemption and personal gifts [234]; and I let love well up in me as I ponder how much our Lord has done for me, and how much he desires to give himself to me. I reflect on my life history so as to bring into focus those ways in which my history of sin has been turned into a graced history by not leaving me to my own devices [58]. My Savior and Redeemer has treated me with loving kindness and compassion [71]. Not only is Jesus "God's gift" (Jn 4: 10) to the world that he loved greatly (Jn 3: 16) but as our glorified Savior he sends us the gift of the Spirit (Jn 19: 30) who gives us life (Jn 6: 63). So much does he love me that even though I take myself away from him, he continues to be my Savior and Redeemer.

All my natural abilities and gifts, along with the gifts of Baptism and the Eucharist and the special graces lavished upon me, are only so many signs of how much God our Lord shares his life with me. My consolation should be that who I am and what I can accomplish for the Kingdom of God is itself a gift of God.

What should I give in return to such a Lover? Moved by love, I may want to express my own love-response in the words so often used by Saint Ignatius who points out [234] that an exercitant can now "make an offering with much feeling."

Take and Receive

Take, Lord, and receive all my liberty,
my memory, my understanding, and my entire will,
all that I have and call my own.
You have given it all to me. To you, Lord, I return it.
Everything is yours; do with it what you will.
Give me only your love and your grace.
That is enough for me.

Day 2 of Week 23: John 14: 6
God gives himself to me.

I reflect that God not only showers me with gifts, but he literally gives himself to me in several different ways [235]. His is not only the Word in whom all things are created, but also the Word who becomes flesh and dwells with us. He strengthens me with food and drink from his own table, the Last Supper, in which he gives his very Body and Blood. As he promised when he left his disciples to go to his Father, Jesus pours out upon me his Spirit of wisdom and love so that I can follow him who is my way to the Father (Jn 14: 6).

God loves me so much that I literally become a dwelling-place or a temple of God—growing in an ever deepening realization that just as the Son can do nothing by himself (Jn 5: 19, 30) so I too share in the "poverty of God's Son," depending on those good gifts from above [237].

Moved by love, I may find that I can respond best in words like "Take and Receive."

Day 3 of Week 23: God labors for me
Jesus answered: "My Father is at work until now, so I am at work."

God loves me so much that he enters into the very struggle of life [236]. We are accustomed to think of God as creating all things and dwelling in everything. But what greater motivation could I have for my life as a laboring contemplative, a contemplative in action, than to recognize that God labors for me? "My Father is at work until now, so I am at work" (Jn 5: 17).

I reflect back to contemplations of the second and third phases in this retreat in which Ignatius draws our attention to the "labor" of Jesus and "the three divine Persons laboring over the Incarnation" [108]. During Jesus' Passion Ignatius asks us to be one with Jesus as we recollect his labors, weariness and sorrows [116, 206]. God labors to share his life and his love. His labors take him even to death on a cross in order to bring forth the life of the Resurrection [219].

Throughout his entire life Jesus serves as a model for our own labors, so that we "may labor and not count the cost." I wish to ponder a thought that Ignatius assumed as a truism, "that love ought to show itself in deeds over and above words" [230].

Reflecting on the many ways that the persons of the Trinity labor for me and for God's Kingdom, what kind of response wells up within me? Let me look again to the prayer, "Take and Receive."

Day 4 of Week 23: God as Giver and Gift
"Look at how all good things and gifts come down from above."

In this fourth and final point of the Contemplation on the love of God, I am led by our glorified Lord into communion with the holy Trinity. Ignatius asks me "to look at how all good things and gifts come down from above," and concludes by suggesting that I should end "by reflecting upon myself" [237]. This last point reaches beyond one's personal life, "to recognize how things speak of him who has given them, who dwells in them, who works in them for the liberation of men. It reaches to a love of God responsive not simply to what he has done, but to what he is in himself." (Buckley, as cited in Stanley, p. 304).

Ignatius, in this Fourth Phase, is pre-eminently concerned with "how the divinity appears and manifests itself so miraculously in the most sacred resurrection through its genuine and most sacred effects" [223]. To drive home this point Ignatius selects several of the most significant effects, "my power, justice, goodness, filial love, mercy" to help me to develop a sense of belonging to the family of God, to help me be aware that all of these effects come from above. "It is uniquely in the heart, the truest part of the self, that one can meet God" (Stanley, p. 305). Jesus' love for me is lavish; he cannot do enough to speak out his love for me--ever calling me to a fuller and better life.

How can I respond to such a generous Giver? Let me consider once again "Take and Receive." I close with an Our Father.

Day 5 of Week 23: God as Giver and Gift:
Immersed in Divinity—I place myself in the Divine Milieu.

Teilhard de Chardin thus expresses God's love for me: "The immensity of God is the essential attribute which allows us to seize him everywhere, within us and around us" (p. 121). Pursuing this in the context of receiving Jesus in the Eucharist, Teilhard expresses a heartfelt COLLOQUY (pp. 127–28).

> "Because you ascended into heaven after having descended into hell, you have so filled the universe in every direction, Jesus, that henceforth it is blessedly impossible for us to escape you. Now I know that for certain. Neither life, whose advance increased your hold upon me; nor death, which throws me into your hands; nor the good or evil spiritual powers which are your living instruments; nor the energies of matter into which you have plunged; nor the irreversible stream of duration whose rhythm and flow you control without appeal; nor the unfathomable abysses of space which are the measure of your greatness—none of these things will be able to separate me from your substantial love, because they are all only the veil, the 'species', under which you take hold of me in order that I may take hold of you.
>
> Sometimes people think that they can increase your attraction in my eyes by stressing almost exclusively the charm and goodness of your human life in the past. But truly, O Lord, if I wanted to cherish only a man, then I would surely turn to those whom you have given me in the allurement of their present flowering. Are there not, with our mothers, brothers, friends and sisters, enough irresistibly lovable people around us? Why should we turn to Judaea two thousand years ago? No, what I cry out for, . . . is a God to adore.
>
> To adore. . .That means to lose oneself in the unfathomable, to plunge into the inexhaustible, to find peace in the incorruptible, to be absorbed in defined immensity, . . . to give of one's deepest to that whose depth has no end. Whom, then, can we adore?
>
> The more man becomes man, the more will he become prey to a need, a need that is always more explicit, more subtle and more magnificent, the need to adore.
>
> Disperse, O Jesus, the clouds with your lightning! Show Yourself to us as the Mighty, the Radiant, the Risen!

Canticle of the Sun

Most high Lord,
Yours are the praises,
The glory and the honors,
And to you alone must be accorded
All graciousness; and no man there
    is who is worthy to name you.

Be praised, O God, and be exalted
My Lord of all creatures,
And in especial of the most high Sun
Which is your creature, O Lord, that
    makes clear
The day and illumines it,
Whence by its fairness and its
    splendor
It is become thy face;
And of the white moon (be praised,
    O Lord)
And of the wandering stars,
Created by you in the heaven
So brilliant and so fair.

Praised be my Lord, by the flame
Whereby night groweth illumined
In the midst of its darkness,
For it is resplendent,
Is joyous, fair, eager; is mighty.

Praised be my Lord, of the air,
Of the winds, of the clear sky,
And of the cloudy, praised
Of all seasons whereby
Live all these creatures
Of lower order.

Praised be my Lord
By our sister the water,
Element meetest for man,
Humble and chaste in its clearness.
Praised be the Lord by our mother
The Earth that sustaineth,
That feeds, that produceth
Multitudinous grasses
And flowers and fruitage.

Praised be my Lord, by those
Who grant pardons through his love,
Enduring their travail in patience
And their infirmity with joy of
    the spirit.

Praised be my Lord by death corporal
Whence escapes no one living.
Woe to those that die in mutual
    transgression
And blessed are they who shall
Find in death's hour thy grace
    that comes
From obedience to thy holy will,
Where through they shall never see
The pain of the death eternal.

Praise and give grace to my Lord
Be grateful and serve him
In humbleness e'en as ye are,
Praise him all creatures!

ST. FRANCIS OF ASSISI
(translated by Ezra Pound)

Week 24: *Totally in His Hands*

Ignatius' ideal, my own; his model, mine: At the close of his Exercises, Ignatius had successfully resolved the problem of his life. The service of God would be his ideal, Jesus Christ his model, the wide world his field of action. For from this moment he would no longer be the solitary pilgrim totally given to meditation and penance, but he would devote all his strength to "the help of souls," that is, to helping others to the fulfillment of their end (de Dalmases, p. 69).

What I want and desire: I ask the Father for an intimate knowledge of the many gifts received so that filled with gratitude for all, I may in all things love and serve the Divine Majesty.

Day 1 of Week 24: Contemplation for attaining love
". . .first is that love ought to be put more in deeds than in words."

Following the guidelines [230-35], I concentrate on the first two focal points, namely: **1)** God's gifts to me, and **2)** God's gift of himself to me as I review the graces and consolations of Phase One.

"The Contemplation for Love is a bridge linking the Exercises with the reality of one's everyday life," as Ignacio Iparraguirre has astutely observed (cited in Stanley, p. 294). Stanley goes on to note that "just as the Principle and Foundation ([23]) was a "presupposition" for entering into the Spiritual Exercises comparable to that of the Prologue to the Fourth Gospel, "so this final contemplation assists the exercitant to channel all the newly acquired energies which have graced the retreat into a dynamic living of the gospel" (p. 294).

Like St. Ignatius, I pray to Jesus' beloved Mother and my spiritual mother that I may be placed with her Son; and that she may be with me in all my labors for his Kingdom. I let my gratitude and love well up as I reflect on these points and conclude with the prayer "Take and Receive."

Day 2 of Week 24: Contemplation for attaining love
". . .second, love consists in interchange between the two."

As on Day 1, review the graces and gifts of Phase Two of the retreat in the light of these two points, deepening still more gratitude, thanksgiving and love [230-35]. Here I "bring to mind the benefits received of creation, redemption, and personal gifts; and to ponder with great love how much God our Lord has done for me, and how much he has given me of what he has, and further, how much the same Lord desires to give himself to me, so far as he can, in accordance with his divine design. And then I will reflect upon myself, by bringing to mind what, in all reason and justice, I ought, on my part, to offer and give to his divine majesty: namely all that I have, and myself as well, like one who makes a gift with all his heart" ([234]). I reflect that both God and I are gifts to each other—God longs to give himself; I long to and am able to offer all that I possess as well as my very self as a complete gift. What a sublime drama: God and mankind drawn to each other in and through all things! Again conclude with "Take and Receive."

Day 3 of Week 24: Contemplation for attaining love
". . .third, to consider how God works and labors for me in all things."

I make the third and fourth focal points, namely: 3) God's labors for me; and 4) God as giver and gift by reviewing the graces and consolations of Phase Three of the retreat [230-33, 236-37].

Ignatius, the ever practical contemplative in action, asks me to reflect on the fact and manner in which God labors for me in all things. The process of discernment being key to making right decisions, we may be confident that Ignatius' goal in this point as in all parts of the Exercises [92, 93, 95, 108, 116, 206, 219] is to energize us to work with and for Jesus. When Jesus cured the man at the Bethesda pool on the Sabbath, he gave as his reason for discerning this controversial course of action, "My Father is at work until now, so I am at work" (Jo 5: 17).

The theme of labor permeates Jesus' life and message. As I see the white fields ripe for harvest, can I doubt that my loving response can be better shown than by sacrificially giving of myself in work? In John's Gospel "Jesus appeals to his 'works' as the authentication of his mission from God (5: 36, 10: 38)", and claims that they are done by the Father in Jesus name (14: 25) and that the Father is at work in him (14: 10).

Day 4 of Week 24: Contemplation for attaining love
". . .fourth, to look how all the good things and gifts descend from above."

I make the fourth point especially by reviewing the graces, gifts and consolations of Phase Four of the retreat, and letting love for the persons of the divine Trinity and my mother, Mary, well up in my heart [230-33, 236-37].

In this point Ignatius "selects certain of the most significant 'effects'" of the manifestation of Jesus' divinity [223] "'my power, justice, goodness, filial love, mercy—for the purpose of assisting the retreatant to acquire that 'sense of family'—the deep awareness of communion through the risen Jesus with the Trinity. Note that in this point my gaze is directed upon those gifts which only I. . .in the depths of my own graced self-awareness. . .can be aware of. . .It is uniquely in 'the heart,' the truest part of the self, that one can meet God, Who in Ignatius' theology is so frequently indicated by the term, 'above' (Stanley, p. 305)." By all of these considerations, Ignatius desires that the retreatant may capture the spirit of the Exercises, also the spirit of the Evangelist John. The mystical insight of Mary Magdalene de Pazzi summed it up: "That spirit consists totally of love and in bringing others to love" (cited by Stanley, p. 309).

And again, I conclude with "Take and Receive."

Day 5 of Week 24: The Prayer of Praise
Place Me With Your Son!

One form of prayer that may help make the presence of the Risen Savior more real in your life and give you a reassuring sense of being supported and surrounded by God's loving providence, is the Prayer of Praise. It can bring you great peace and joy. This simple form of prayer consists of thanking and of praising God for everything whatever in your life. Its basis is the belief that nothing happens in your life that is not, or at least cannot be turned to God's glory—absolutely nothing, not even your sins--not even the the murder of Jesus Christ.

When you have repented, you can praise God even for your sins because he will draw great good from them. Saint Paul encourages his disciples the Romans as follows, "Where sin increased, grace overflowed all the more." Again, he said, "What then shall we say? Shall we persist in sin that grace may abound? Of course not" (Rom. 5:20; 6:1). But having given thanks to God for your sins and his deliverance from them, you can learn to praise God for them. Peter surely repented his denial of Jesus and the fact that he was too weak to be a source of support to Jesus on his way to Calvary.

Too often people carry a lifelong burden of guilt in their hearts for sins they have committed. Even when convinced of God's forgiveness, many are unable to shake off their feeling of guilt. If you can express heartfelt thanks and praise to God for having sinned, you may feel that all is well, that all is in God's hands, and that your labors will be fruitful as a result.

With this consideration in mind, recall some event from the past or present that causes you guilt, distress, frustration or pain. If you were actually blameworthy, express to your risen Lord your feelings of regret and sorrow. Go on to explicitly thank God and praise him for it, confidently telling him that you believe that even this can help in some way to make you a more effective instrument in his service.

Leave this distress and all the other events of your life, past, present, and future, in God's hands, and savor the peace and relief that may arise. Your attitude will then be that of St. Paul, "forgetting what lies behind but straining forward to what lies ahead, I continue my pursuit toward the goal, the prize of God's upward calling, in Christ Jesus" (Phil 3: 13-14). And "the peace of God that surpasses all understanding will guard your hearts and minds in Christ Jesus" (Phil. 4:7).

That sense of peace and joy will become a habitual disposition with you as you thank God in every circumstance of your life. Thus your life will be full of the love that comes to you from above and you can again say with Ignatius of Loyola from the depths of your heart [234M]:

Take Lord, and receive all my liberty,
my memory, my understanding, and my entire will,
all that I have and call my own.
You have given it all to me. To you, Lord, I return it.
Everything is yours; do with it what you will.
Give me only your love and your grace.
That is enough for me.

Resources for the Study of the Spiritual Exercises

BIBLIOGRAPHY

Begheyn, Paul. "A Bibliography on St. Ignatius' *Spiritual Exercises*: A Working-Tool for American Students." *Studies in the Spirituality of Jesuits*. 13.2 , American Assistancy Seminar on Jesuit Spirituality, St. Louis: 1981.

TEXTS OF THE EXERCISES

Fleming, David L. *The Spiritual Exercises of St. Ignatius. A Literal Translation and a Contemporary Reading*. St. Louis: Institute of Jesuit Sources, 244 pp. 1980.

Puhl, Louis J. *The Spiritual Exercises of St. Ignatius: Based on Studies in the Language of the Autograph*. Chicago: Loyola University Press, 1951.

OTHER WRITINGS BY IGNATIUS

The Autobiography of Saint Ignatius Loyola with Related Documents. Translated by Joseph F. O'Callaghan and edited by John C. Olin. New York: Harper & Row, 1974.

The Constitutions of the Society of Jesus. Translated and edited by George E. Ganss. St. Louis: The Institute of Jesuit Sources, 1970.

The Pilgrim's Journey: The Autobiography of Ignatius of Loyola. Translation and commentary by Joseph N. Tylenda. Wilmington, Del.: Michael Glazier, 1985.

The Spiritual Journal of St. Ignatius of Loyola. Translated by William J. Young. Rome: Centrum Ignatianum Spiritualitatis, 1974.

COMMENTARIES ON THE EXERCISES

Coathalem, Harvé. *Ignatian Insights. A Guide to the Complete Spiritual Exercises*. Translated by Charles J. McCarthy, 2d ed. Taichung, Taiwan: Kuangchi Press, 1971.

Cowan, Marian, and John Futrell. *The Spiritual Exercises of St. Ignatius of Loyola: A Handbook for Directors*, New York: Le Jacq Publishing, 1982.

English, John. *Spiritual Freedom: From an Experience of the Ignatian Exercises to the Art of Spiritual Direction*. Guelph, Ontario: Loyola House, 1973.

Peters, William A. *The Spiritual Exercises of St. Ignatius: Exposition and Interpretation*. 2d ed. Rome: Centrum Ignatianum Spiritualitatis, 1978.

Stanley, David M. *"I Encountered God!" The Spiritual Exercises with the Gospel of Saint John*. 328 pp. St. Louis: The Institute of Jesuit Sources, 1986.

Tetlow, Joseph. *Choosing Christ in the World: Directing the Spiritual Exercises of St. Ignatius According to Annotations Eighteen and Nineteen*. Handbook, 254 pp. St. Louis: The Institute of Jesuit Sources, 1989.

BIOGRAPHIES OF IGNATIUS

de Dalmases, Cándido. *Ignatius of Loyola, Founder of the Jesuits: His Life and Work*. St. Louis: The Institute of Jesuit Sources, 1985.

Egan, Harvey D. *Ignatius Loyola the Mystic* in The Way of the Christian Mystics, vol 5, 229 pp. Wilmington, Del.: Michael Glazier, 1987.

STUDIES AND EXPLICATIONS OF IGNATIAN SPIRITUALITY

Aschenbrenner, George A. "Consciousness Examen." St. Louis: *Review for Religious*, 31 (1972), 14-21.

Barry, William A., "The Experience of the First and Second Weeks of the Spiritual Exercises" in *Review for Religious*, 32 (1973), 102-109. Reprinted under the same title with Fleming, D. L., ed. (1973), "Notes on the Spiritual Exercises of St. Ignatius of Loyola." St. Louis: *Review for Religious*.

Brou, Alexandre. *Ignatian Methods of Prayer*. Translated by William J. Young. Milwaukee: Bruce, 1949.

Egan, Harvey. *The Spiritual Exercises and the Ignatian Mystical Horizon*. St. Louis: The Institute of Jesuit Sources, 1976.

Futrell, John C. "Ignatian Discernment". *Studies in the Spirituality of Jesuits* II/2, 1970.

Green, Thomas H. *Weeds Among the Wheat. Discernment: Where Prayer and Action Meet*. Notre Dame, Ind.: Ave Maria Press, 1984.

Hassel, David J. *Radical Prayer*. New York/Ramsey: Paulist Press, 1982

Metz, Johannes. *Poverty of Spirit*. Paramus, N. J.: Paulist Press, 1968.

Rahner, Hugo. *Ignatius the Theologian*. New York: Herder and Herder, 1968.

Sheldrake, Philip. "Imagination and Prayer." *The Way*. 24 (1984), 92-102.

Whelan, Joseph. "Jesuit Apostolic Prayer." *The Way*. Supplement #19 (1973), 13-21.

OTHER REFERENCES

Abbott, Walter M., ed., Decree on the Apostolate of the Laity in *The Documents of Vatican II*, pp. 489- 521. New York: Guild Press, 1966.

Bergant, Dianne and R. J. Karris, eds., *The Collegeville Bible Commentary (CBC). Based on the New American Bible with Revised New Testament*, 1301 pp. Collegeville, Minn.: The Liturgical Press, 1989.

Brown, R. E., J. A. Fitzmyer, and R. E. Murphy, eds. *The New Jerome Biblical Commentary (NJBC)*. 1475 pp. Englewood Cliffs, N.J.: Prentice Hall, 1990.

Documents of the 31st and 32nd General Congregations of the Society of Jesus. An English translation of the offical Latin texts and the accompanying Papal Documents, 598 pp. St. Louis: The Institute of Jesuit Sources, 1977.

Documents of the 33rd General Congregation of the Society of Jesus. An English translation of the official Latin texts and Related Documents, 115 pp. St. Louis: The Institute of Jesuit Sources, 1984.

King, T. M. , *Teilhard's Mysticism of Knowing*, 154 pp. New York: The Seabury Press, 1981.

Teilhard de Chardin, Pierre, *Hymn of the Universe*, 158 pp., New York: Harper & Row, 1961.

____. *Writings in Time of War*, 315 pp., New York: Harper & Row, 1968.

____. *The Divine Milieu*. 160 pp. New York: Harper & Row, Harper Colophon Books, 1968.

de Mello, Anthony. *Sadhana: A Way to God*. Christian Exercises in Eastern Form. 134 pp. St. Louis: The Institute of Jesuit Sources, 1987.

Calendar for the Spiritual Exercises as an ISEL Retreat

Ignatian Spirituality in Everyday Life

PHASE ONE OF THE EXERCISES   *Beginning Date*

    Week 1: *Soul of Christ, sanctify me*   (p. 18)   _____

    Week 2: *The Principle and Foundation*   (p. 24)   _____

    Week 3: *Sin and the Great Struggle*   (p. 31)   _____

    Week 4: *A Sinner loved by God*   (p. 38)   _____

PHASE TWO OF THE EXERCISES

    Week 5: *The Call and the Coming of the Eternal King*   (p. 49)   _____

    Week 6: *The Incarnation and Birth of Jesus*   (p. 57)   _____

    Week 7: *The "Showing Forth" of the Newborn King*   (p. 64)   _____

    Week 8: *The Hidden Life of Jesus*   (p. 71)   _____

    Week 9: *The Strategy of Jesus*   (p. 77)   _____

    Week 10: *The Mission Begins*   (p. 83)   _____

    Week 11: *Jesus Calls Me by Name*   (p. 87)   _____

    Week 12: *Jesus Teaches Me with Words of "Power and Light"*   (p. 93)   _____

    Week 13: *Jesus Heals Me*   (p. 98)   _____

    Week 14: *Jesus Challenges Me*   (p. 102)   _____

    Week 15: *Jesus Nurtures Me with Words of "Power and Light"*   (p. 109)   _____

    Week 16: *Jesus Accepts and Bestows Love*   (p. 114)   _____

PHASE THREE OF THE EXERCISES

    Week 17: *Jesus is Betrayed*   (p. 123)   _____

    Week 18: *Jesus Suffers Injustices, Insults, and Torture*   (p. 130)   _____

    Week 19: *The King Mounts His Throne of Glory*   (p. 134)   _____

PHASE FOUR OF THE EXERCISES

    Week 20: *Christ the Lord Conquers Death*   (p. 142)   _____

    Week 21: *The King Sends Forth His Followers*   (p. 145)   _____

    Week 22: *Another Advocate [Paraclete]*   (p. 149)   _____

    Week 23: *The Prodigal God: Contemplation on Love*   (p. 153)   _____

    Week 24: *Totally in His Hands*   (p. 158)   _____